Movie Publicity Showcase
Volume 28

Buster Keaton's

"The General"
and "Steamboat Bill, Jr."

I. Joseph Hyatt

DEDICATION

To all the people who worked on the films in front of and behind the cameras. To all the people who worked in the offices creating the publicity. To all the people that helped in the distribution and exhibition of this movie. To all the people working today to preserve and make available classic films to the public.

To the members of the Sons of the Desert for helping to keep the films of Laurel and Hardy alive.

To my wife Mary who has put up with my old movie obsession all these years. To Dave Lord Heath for all his emotional support and his creation of his website "Another Fine Mess" (www.lordheath.com). To Mark Eisler, a good and true friend. To John K. Carpenter whose passion for Charley Chase, Laurel and Hardy and Buster Keaton is never ending.

Finally, to an unknown Fireman from the Iselin, New Jersey firehouse who showed me that it was possible to own a print of a movie for home use (see introduction). I am sure he never realized the influence he had on a 9-year-old child. That Christmas my mother and father bought me my first home movie projector and collecting film and movie memorabilia is still my hobby over six decades later.

<u>INTRODUCTION</u>
(Reprinted from Volume 1 in the Movie Publicity Showcase series)

For many "old time" movie fans that grew up in the sixties and seventies, television gave us our first exposure to classic films. In a day before video tape recorders, cable, streaming, DVD, Blu-ray, and computers we considered ourselves lucky when one of our favorite movies was broadcast. With the exception of the CBS annual broadcast of "The Wizard of Oz" and stations such as New York's WOR that ran one movie (Million Dollar Movie) eleven times a week, an average movie would probably air twice in a five-year period.

However there was an exception. A large one, mainly aimed for a children's audience. You could find movie series like "The East Side Kids/Bowery Boys", "Laurel and Hardy", "Abbott and Costello" and low budget horror movies weekly airing every Saturday. Under group titles such as "East Side Comedy" or "Chiller Theater" weekly showings of many of these favorites were more visible than the serious or classic films.

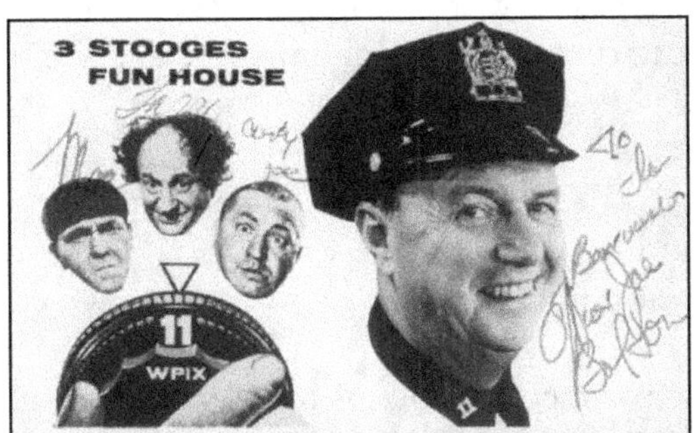

WPIX's Officer Joe Bolton presented the Three Stooges daily.

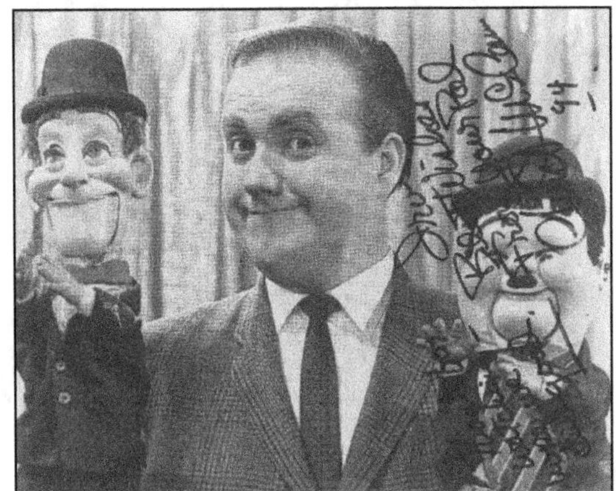

Chuck McCann with the Paul Ashley Puppets.

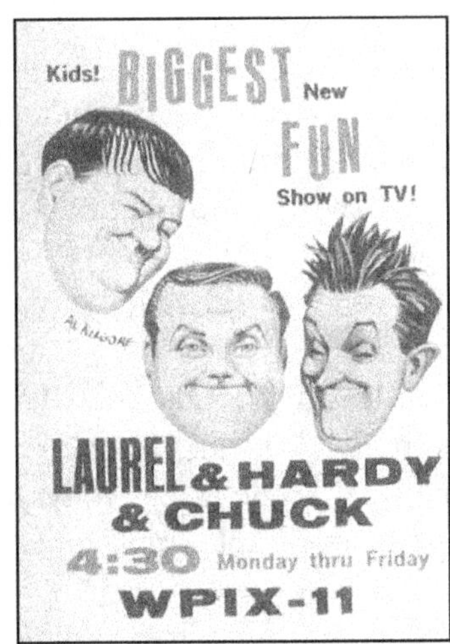

Early ad for Chuck McCann's daily show.

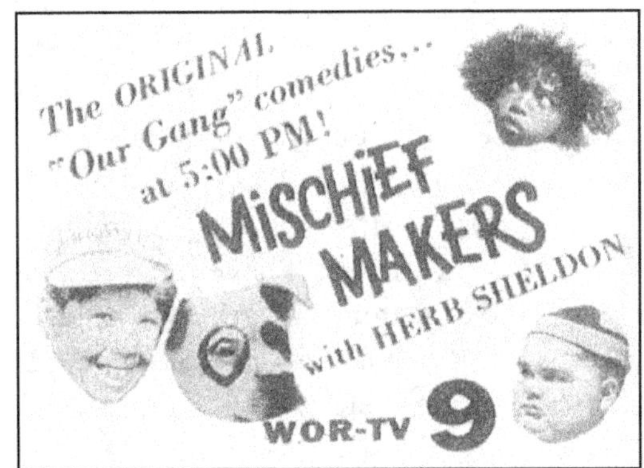

The Little Rascals/Our Gang were funny under any name.

Making the rounds of TV stations during this same period were a number of movie shorts collections, the most visible of these clusters being the Three Stooges, Laurel and Hardy and the Little Rascals/Our Gang. On many stations they were run with a live host. Chuck McCann, "Officer" Joe Bolton, Alan Swift and John Zacherley were hosts in the New York/New Jersey market. Other cities across the country had their own local hosts. Often these shows would broadcast Monday through Friday, and appear on the weekends as well.

Since we could not own a copy of the film as you can today, many of us tried to "capture" a bit of the emotions we felt by buying magazines, comics, toys, photos, and records with our favorite movie personalities. Sound tracks were recorded on our reel-to-reel audio tape recorders. Some of us even had a family home movie projector where you could buy a few minutes of older films and cartoons in 8mm silent (later sound) editions for a reasonable price (if we saved up our money and Dad let us use the family projector). For most of us, a more professional film gauge was just an expensive dream.

Now collectables like movie posters, photos, and other movie memorabilia are very expensive. Back in the 1960's and earlier theaters and movie distributors would recycle posters, photos and movie campaign books until the films reached the end of their theatrical showings. Then these paper items would be disposed of. The suppliers (like National Cinema Service) either threw out or gave these mementoes to anyone who would clear their warehouse. Stores like Marc Ricci's Memory Shop in New York City and many more acquired much of this material by the truckload. Before these items were considered collectable (or even worthy of preservation) we could purchase some of these photos, lobby cards, and posters between $1 - $7 each in stores like this, or through mail order.

Today many posters sell in the 5 and 6 figures range. Pre-1940 material is the most expensive, since many of the paper items were donated (and recycled) for the war effort. Today it takes a collector with "deep pockets" to afford some of the original material.

For movie lovers and students of film one of these prize collectables is the movie campaign book. Originally campaign books, more commonly referred to as "press books", were circulated to theaters during the film's distribution. They were used so the movie exhibitor could pick out the posters that would fit his theater front and to choose pre-written articles and ads to run in newspapers within the theater's advertising budget.

Without trying, press books ended up documenting the choice of posters, banners, photos and other promotional items that were available at the time of release for future generations to see. Radio ads, ideas for lobby displays, publicity articles, newspaper ad artwork, and general information about the film were also documented and preserved within its pages.

This series of books, starting with "Movie Publicity Showcase - Volume One - Laurel and Hardy in Swiss Miss", have been put together to allow people to understand what it was like to be a patron (or theater manager) when these films were originally presented. It is also a source for other film students, writers, or the movie enthusiast to read items (some fact- some Hollywood fiction at its finest) that were written to make an audience desire to be in the movie's audience.

Most of the press books in this series are presented as they were originally printed with two exceptions. A common size for these press books was approximately 12" x 18" in size. While full pages were used to represent the cover, back and poster pages, articles had to be separated and enlarged to make reading possible in this 8.5" x 11" book format. The synopsis covering the story (which included the ending) has also been eliminated. These synopsizes were not intended for use in publicizing the movie and give away the total story, including the ending.

Many archives and movie studios are now actively restoring and preserving the remaining film and advertising elements that still exist today. Please support these intuitions and corporations.

INTRODUCTION TO MOVIE PUBLICITY SHOWCASE VOLUME 28
BUSTER KEATON'S "THE GENERAL" AND "STEAMBOAT BILL, JR."

So much has been written about Buster Keaton and his two top films: "The General" and "Steamboat Bill, Jr." "Movie Publicity Showcase – Volume 28" adds the original release pressbooks to the available material on Keaton.

Many film and memorabilia collectors have stories on how and why they became fans of Buster Keaton. Here is how it happened to me.

I Have been hooked on old movies since I was very young. They were a part of our daily television diet. Clips of silent movies were used as punchlines in children's programing such as the Soupy Sales Show and Howdy Doody and sometimes you could catch a film on "The Joe Franklin Show" which was closer to complete. Most of these films were poor murky dupes and while funny, they were hard to appreciate in that form.

At the age of 9 years old, my father read about a local fireman who was showing a "summer film series" for the neighborhood kids. He knew I enjoyed these films so on Saturdays, in the summer of 1962, my Dad would drive me to the neighboring town to see these movies.

While I enjoyed the matinees at our own town's State Theater, these film shows were different. First, the venue was the firehouse itself. The engines were moved out and folding chairs were set up. A local fireman was a 16mm movie collector. He had a large screen and his projector was set up in the back of the room.

The first movie I ever saw there was W.C. Fields in "Million Dollar Legs." The following week the fireman ran a "Flash Gordon" feature. The third week he ran Buster Keaton's "Steamboat Bill, Jr."

It was my first exposure to a nice clear copy of a silent (with music track} Keaton film. I was mesmerized. I begged my parents to buy me a small 8mm home movie projector that Christmas. I discovered local department stores sold movies, some as low as 89c. I also discovered my addiction. Celluloid.

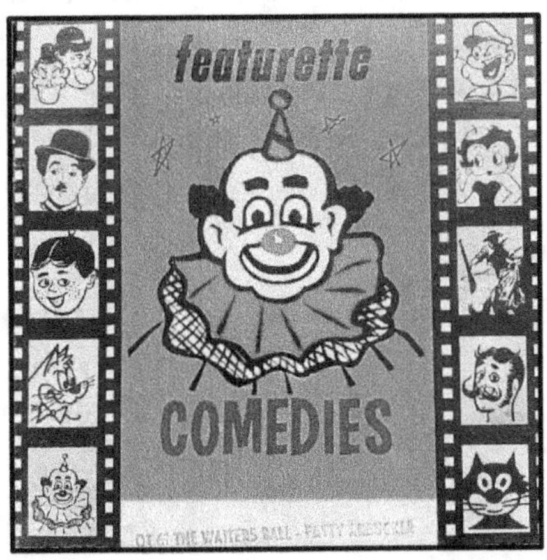

This is a three-minute condensation of Arbuckle's "The Waiters Ball." Originally from 1916 this film was the one of the Atlas 89c films I purchased in the 1960's. Keaton joined Arbuckle the following year in "The Butcher Boy," a 1917 short.

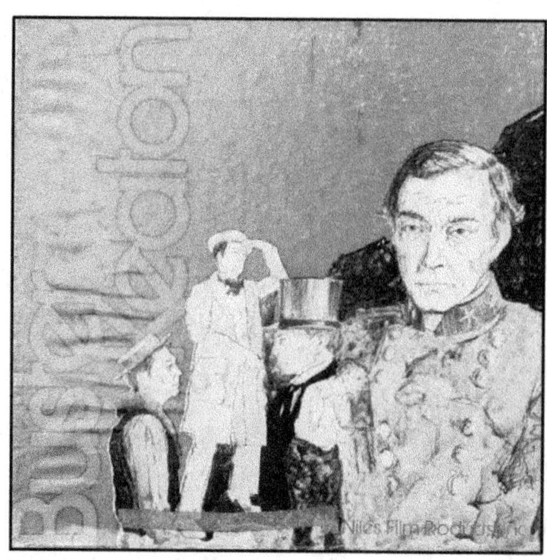

Niles Film, another film manufacturer, released the feature "The General" in 8mm as well as in 16mm. Their quality was better than Atlas and they offered the full uncut feature. When showing these to our friends, we would use records as background music.

It took me years to step up to a "professional" 16mm projector and to find good prints of "The General" and "Steamboat Bill. Jr." Buster Keaton was incredible, and his work holds up nearly 100 years after their production.

I also became hooked on posters and pressbooks. Back in the 60's these items were low cost, unlike today. As an example: I paid $6.00 for my Laurel and Hardy one-sheet for "Great Guns" and $7.00 for the pressbook of the same title.

"Movie Publicity Showcase Volume 28" reproduces the original 1926 and 1928 pressbooks for "The General" and "Steamboat Bill, Jr.". There is some yellowing and some imperfections to be found within these pages and some minor editing was done where an article was damaged. These pressbooks are over 96 years old.

The pictures and articles here will hopcfully bring you back to a time when these movies were first released. If you are into serious research, or just reading these for the pure enjoyment, make sure to see these movies (if you have not already!). Both are available in pristine prints along with most of Keaton's prime work. While both films are distributed in low-cost editions, it is worth the additional cost to purchase licensed restorations in either DVD or Blu-ray for the picture quality alone. Kino, Cohen, and Criterion product almost look like they were filmed yesterday and all are available at the time of this writing.

"The General" and "Steamboat Bill, Jr." are two of the greatest motion pictures ever made!

I. Joseph Hyatt
March 3, 2024

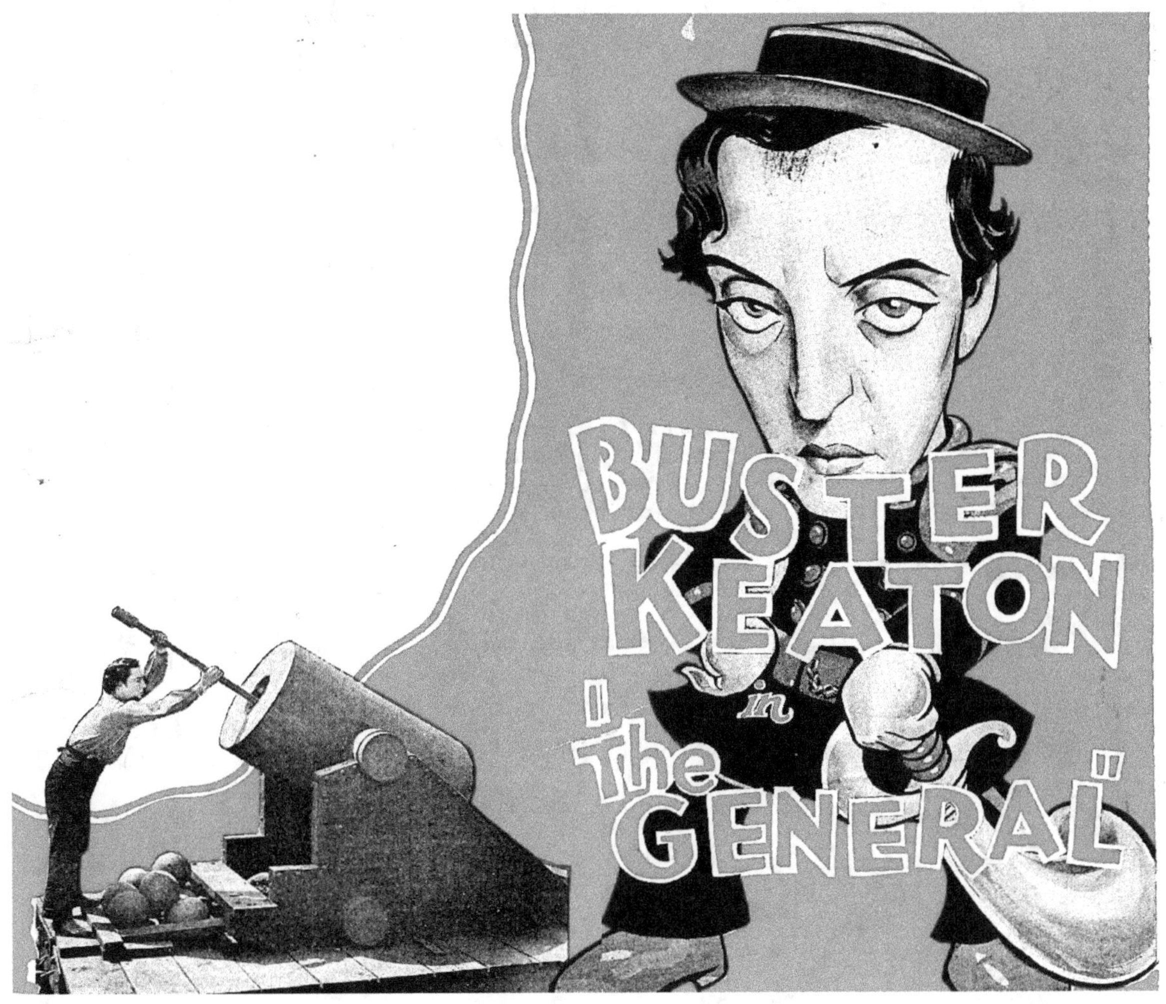

Buster Keaton's "The General" (1926)

Feature Film

75 Minutes

Original Release Pressbook

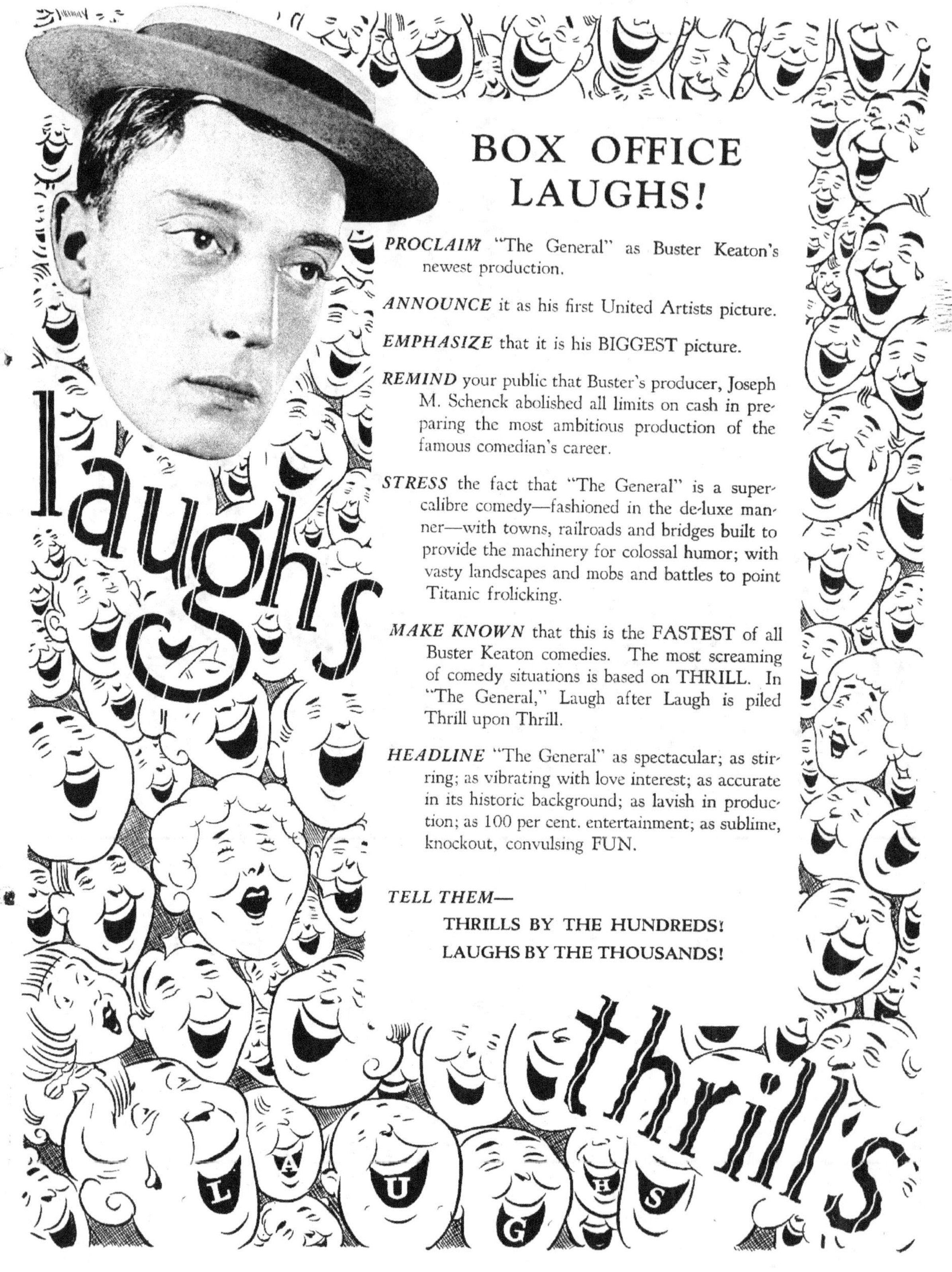

laughs

BOX OFFICE
LAUGHS!

PROCLAIM "The General" as Buster Keaton's
newest production.

ANNOUNCE it as his first United Artists picture.

EMPHASIZE that it is his BIGGEST picture.

REMIND your public that Buster's producer, Joseph
M. Schenck abolished all limits on cash in preparing the most ambitious production of the
famous comedian's career.

STRESS the fact that "The General" is a super-
calibre comedy—fashioned in the de-luxe manner—with towns, railroads and bridges built to
provide the machinery for colossal humor; with
vasty landscapes and mobs and battles to point
Titanic frolicking.

MAKE KNOWN that this is the FASTEST of all
Buster Keaton comedies. The most screaming
of comedy situations is based on THRILL. In
"The General," Laugh after Laugh is piled
Thrill upon Thrill.

HEADLINE "The General" as spectacular; as stirring; as vibrating with love interest; as accurate
in its historic background; as lavish in production; as 100 per cent. entertainment; as sublime,
knockout, convulsing FUN.

TELL THEM—
THRILLS BY THE HUNDREDS!
LAUGHS BY THE THOUSANDS!

thrills

LAUGHS

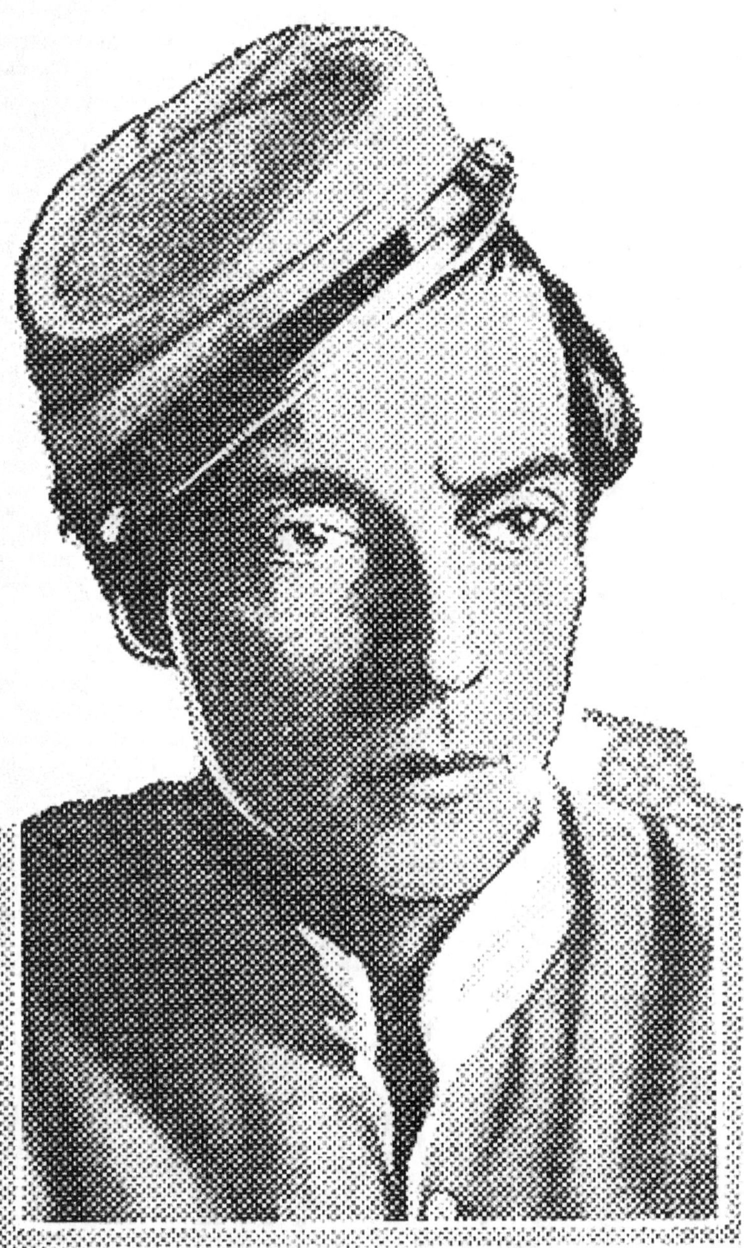

BK 5—One Col.
Scene (Cut 30c Mat 5c)

JOSEPH M. SCHENCK
presents
BUSTER KEATON
in
"THE GENERAL"
**Adapted by Al Boasberg and
Charles Smith**

**Photographed by J. D. Jennings
and Bert Haines**

Fred Gabourie, technical editor;
Denver Harmon, electrical effects; J. S. Kell, film editor;
Harry Barnes, assistant director.

**Directed by Buster Keaton and
Clyde Bruckman**

United Artists Picture

THE CAST
Johnnie Gray............Buster Keaton
Captain Anderson..Glenn Cavender
General Thatcher............Jim Farley
A Southern General,
                    Frederick Vroom
Annabelle Lee..........Marian Mack
Her Father................Charles Smith
Her Brother..............Frank Barnes
Three Union Officers..Joe Keaton
                                Mike Donlin
                                Tom Nawn

WHAT IT'S ALL ABOUT

In 1862 there were thousands of patriots, both northerners and southerners, who chafed under the tasks imposed upon them by their respective governments. Many of them, yearning for glory in the first line of fighting, were doomed to serve in less heroic capacities.

One of these unsung heroes—unsung in 1862—was a young southerner (Buster Keaton), who repeatedly tried to enlist in the Confederate army, but who was refused on the ground that he was of more value to the cause as the engineer of "The General." (In those days the crack railway locomotives were known by names instead of numbers.)

The youth didn't particularly care because his bravery was questioned by his friends in the south; he knew he was doing his duty and serving in the capacity that the military chieftains decreed; what hurt him was that his sweetheart, too, believed he was a slacker, unwilling to don the gray uniform of the army. So, after being rejected by the sweetest girl in Dixie, Buster turned to his only friend, "The General."

The engine was his pride and joy and he gloried in grooming it as if it were a human giant. Spurned by the girl he loved and sneered at by the southern fire-eaters, who imagined that the only way a man could serve his country was to shoulder a musket and meet the enemy hand to hand, the youth lived with and for his beloved.

Only the highest men in the army knew that he would rather enlist than remain with "The General" as pilot; the people of the south—and his sweetheart—insisted that the railroad job was merely a subterfuge to escape military service.

In April of 1862 there occurred one of the most thrilling and history making events of the struggle between the states. It was the famous Andrews railroad raid, when a score of Union daredevils captured the locomotive, "The General," at Big Shanty, Georgia, hoping to make their way to Chattanooga, burning bridges and tearing up the track behind them, in an attempt to prevent the southern army from succoring the Tennessee city.

The young engineer, braving death and capture, started in pursuit of the raiders, not so much as a duty to the south, but to rescue his iron friend and companion, "The General." Then followed one of the perilous chapters of the Civil War.

Keeping so closely on the heels of the northerners that they were prevented from carrying out their bridge burning plans, the youth eventually found himself inside the Federal lines and a prisoner.

On the same train with the youth, but unbeknown to him, was his sweetheart, who happened to be in the baggage car looking for her trunk when the raid started. She, too, was taken prisoner, and she believed Buster's appearance on the scene was to rescue her from the Yanks.

After a series of exciting and laughable—to some one else, not him—adventures in the northern camp, Buster managed to escape with the girl, re-captured his locomotive, and started back for the southern lines. While a prisoner of the Federal forces, he had learned of plans for a surprise attack on the Confederates. Fleeing toward home with his sweetheart and "The General," he unconsciously blocked the progress of the northern forces long enough to give warning to the Confederate leaders.

This adventure was looked upon as a tremendous service to the south. Acclaimed as a hero and idolized by the former friends who had shunned him, Buster was then permitted to enlist, being appointed a lieutenant in the Confederate army.

And, of course, the girl forgave him and welcomed him to her arms as a real southern hero.

"The General" was produced by Joseph M. Schenck on an extremely big scale. Keaton and his staff spent months in research work, traveling thousands of miles in their hunt for historical data.

Although primarily for laughing purposes, the picture is historically accurate and does not in any way burlesque the days of '62. Instead, a serious attempt has been made to re-enact some of the most thrilling lighter chapters of the great conflict.

Thousands of extras were recruited to play the parts of northern and southern soldiers and citizens of that part of the south in which the celebrated railroad raid took place. Many miles of specially built railroad were utilized. Several old locomotives were rebuilt into engines of the type used during the Civil War and scores of technically perfect passenger coaches and freight cars constructed.

"The General" is Keaton's first United Artists picture and it was directed by the star himself and Clyde Bruckman.

BOOST BUSTER KEATON

WEDDING PHOTOS

Invite the public to enter old-time bride-and-groom portraits in a contest; call for "Daguerreotypes of the '60's"; offer prizes for the quaintest poses and costumes; or for costumes most closely resembling those used in "The General." Let Still No. 17 be your guide.

Get newspaper cooperation on the old daguerreotype contest. Such a contest promises great reader interest as well as novelty.

Get a loan collection of old tintypes or daguerreotype subjects for a window or for a lobby display, especially tintypes that are contest entries. Feature the contest in every way.

Make slides or film shots of the winning tintypes and flash them on the screen for your audiences. Or, you can develop this screen idea by having the audience make the decisions from the entries flashed on the screen.

Handle this contest in a dignified manner, and press home the fact that the old portraits had high artistic merit despite the fact that the costumes look odd to the present generation.

"FROZEN FACES"

Go in for a "Frozen Face Contest." Call for candidates to rival Buster Keaton's impassivity under any circumstances. Hang up prizes for those men or women who can keep a straight face when everyone is trying to make them laugh or smile.

Handle this like an "Amateur Night"—having your contestants on the stage while the audience good-naturedly "razzes" them. The first contestant who laughs or grins at one of the audience's "wise cracks" is eliminated, and so on until the most stoical one remains. Have the orchestra help along with grotesque medleys of standard and ragtime airs.

You can combine a newspaper competition for stony-faced photographs with personal appearances in the "Frozen Face Contest."

An ice cream eating contest can be combined with the "Frozen Face Contest." Let your contestants freeze their "Frozen Faces" by eating ice cream on the stage while the audience tries to make them laugh. Ice cream should be supplied by some local dealers for the ad.

LAUGHTER CARD

Make up an imitation labor union membership card for special distribution. It should be made out to Joseph F. (Buster) Keaton, as a member in good standing in the "Brotherhood of Laughtermotive Engineers"; address, your theatre; employed, on the W & A. R. R.; local lodge, "The General"; dues paid up, to date of your opening; etc.

You might also plant cards of this kind and offer rewards for their return, conducting a treasure hunt.

Distribute these "Laughter-Motive Union Cards" to all local lodges in your town, having them handed out on meeting nights to individual members.

If you can get a mailing list of lodge members, mail them out direct.

RAILROADING

Railroad offices will cooperate with you in displaying photographs and models of their older equipment, along with atmosphere stills from "The General," and with models and photographs of their modern rolling stock as a contrast.

"HOW TO FIRE A CANNON"-Posed by BUSTER KEATON in "THE GENERAL"

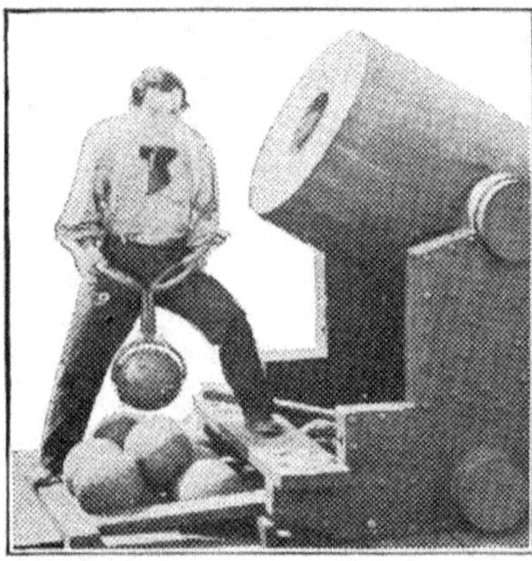

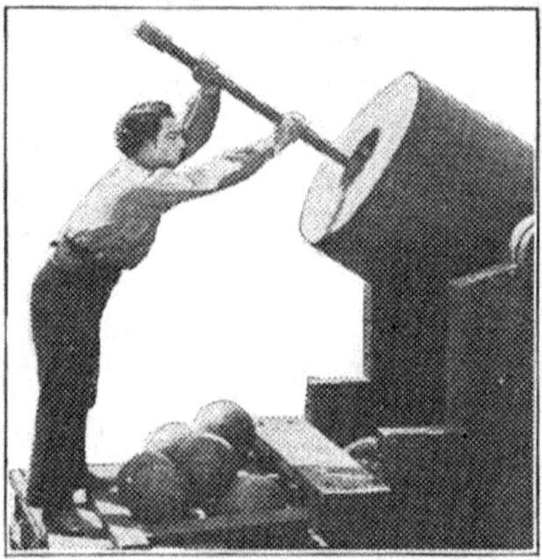

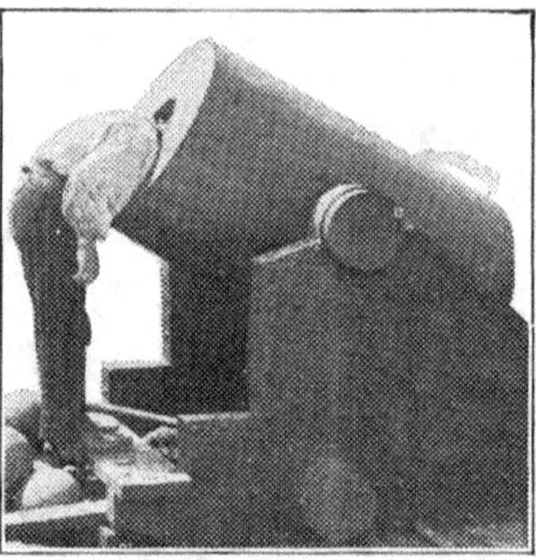

LOADING—Obtain ammunition at a bowling alley—round shot, shrapnel, pretzels, Edam cheeses—anything! Procure a pair of rubber ice tongs that will not scratch the enamel. You have already packed the bore of the cannon with T. N. T. and apple sauce. Lift in shot. Wad same with a clean undershirt and some Chinese laundry tickets.	RAMMING—Push the charge home with a dustless mop. If no mop is available, use a crutch. Save the crutch—you'll need it. For the sake of an accurate shot be sure and chalk the tip of the crutch. See that all dampers are open. Make your will. Before doing that, however, kiss the cook.	FIRING—Shake all the old ashes out of the grate so that cannon will have a good draft. Insert short fuse into firebox and touch fuse with a match. Use a lot of matches; use two. Tune in your radio for angel music. Look into muzzle to see if T. N. T. has caught. If it has, you will hear beautiful singing and see visions of Venus doing the Charleston.

For this newspaper feature get BK-11— Four-Column Cannon MATS ONLY (Mat 30 Cents)

HOW I BROKE INTO THE MOVIES

By BUSTER KEATON
(Star of "The General at the . . . . Theatre)

Having spent twenty-one years on the stage, as a member of The Three Keatons, and having reached the ripe old age of twenty-one, I decided to make a change. This was about a decade ago.

Father, mother and I had played all over the world. An offer to leave the variety stage and appear in a Shubert revue at the Winter Garden meant that I was to go "on my own" for the first time. And I was to receive seven hundred and fifty—count 'em—dollars a week!

It was while awaiting rehearsals that I ran into a twist of fate which altered the whole course of my life. I was introduced to Joseph M. Schenck, who said he was making some two-reel comedies, and he offered me an opportunity to try my luck in the pictures. "Salary?" Forty dollars a week.

There was—and is—a lot of difference between $750 a week and $40 a week. I don't know why I decided against the fat salary. Perhaps it was because I was afraid I couldn't find use for that much money, and perhaps— and this is really the real reason—because I had been traveling since the day I was born, and the prospect of settling down in one place for a time looked marvelously inviting.

I'll admit I didn't have any idea that pictures would develop into what they are today; in my wildest fancy I didn't envision myself as a star.

Anyway, I accepted Mr. Schenck's offer.

The first picture I worked in was called, "The Butcher Boy." Part of the business was for two comedians to toss bags of flour at each other. I got in the way of one of the bags, and was knocked colder than an Eskimo sleeping porch. Then later in the scene I got myself well lathered with molasses. When the day's work was finished I was more than a terrible mess—I was a wreck!

And for a life like this I had sacrificed $70 a week!

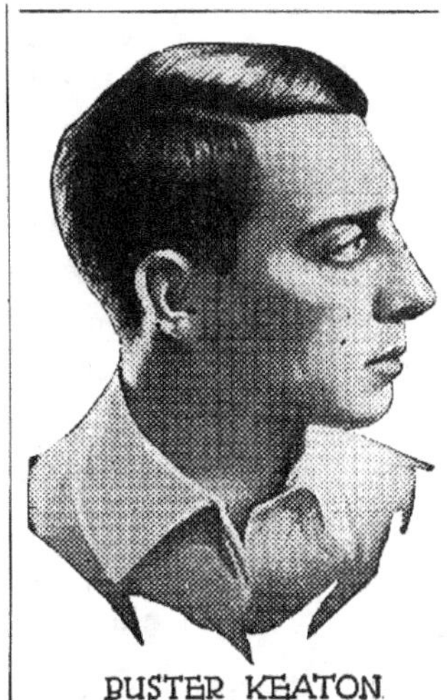

BUSTER KEATON

BK-1—One Col. Portrait
Cut 30c; Mat 5c
BK-2—Two Col. Portrait.
Cut 50c; Mat 10c

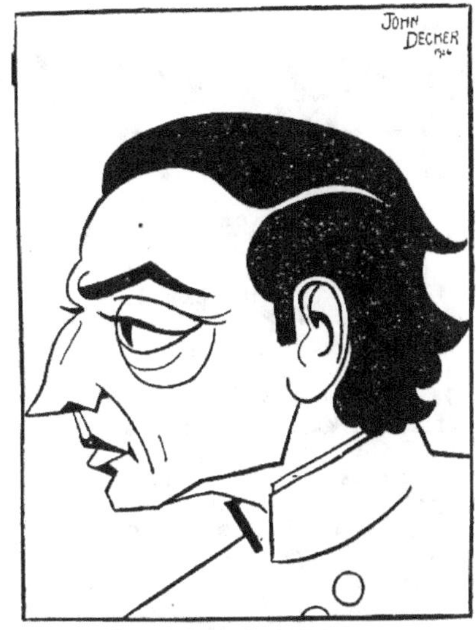

BK-3—One Col. Sketches
4 on Mat 10c

KEATON PICKED SOLDIERS FOR SOLDIER PARTS

When Buster Keaton cast the principals in "The General," his million dollar comedy of the Civil War, which is the feature at the....................Theatre, he chose, so far as possible, actors who had served in the military forces of the United States.

Keaton himself served for eighteen months overseas during the World War, and dozens of others in the huge United Artists laugh feature, produced by Joseph M. Schenck, are veterans of the army and navy. One of these supporting players, who was personally selected by Buster because of his army record and his wide experience in motion pictures, is Glen Cavender.

There are few men in pictures who have had more colorful careers than Cavender has participated in several wars, and he holds many medals, among them the Congressional Medal, America's highest military decoration.

More than a quarter of a century ago, when he was a member of the Sixth U. S. Cavalry, Cavender won the Congressional Medal, the Medal for Valor and the Medal for Conspicuous Bravery Under Fire for his feats during the Philippine campaign and in the Chinese Boxer expedition. He was decorated by France with the medal of a Chevalier Legion d'Honour for conspicuous bravery at Peking when he saved the life of a French marshal.

Cavender retired from the army in 1907 and pioneered in motion pictures, both as a director and as a featured player.

The World War found the retired army man back in the thick of the fighting. As a major in the Officers' Reserve Corps, Cavender was called to the colors and served in the intelligence department. One of his feats during the World War was to capture, single-handed, two high officers of the German army and bring them through the American lines. For this service he was again decorated by the United States and French Governments and also by Italy.

Cavender was a personal friend of the late Theodore Roosevelt, and served on the future President's staff during the Spanish-American War. He was chosen by President Roosevelt as the army officer to serve as Alice Roosevelt's personal bodyguard when the executive's daughter visited the Philippines.

Directed by the comedy star himself, "The General," his first United Artists picture, employs the services of thousands of people and introduces great masses of Civil War equipment, such as three authentic locomotives and scores of 1861 passenger coaches and freight cars. One of the engines plunges through a burning trestle to furnish a $40,000 one-minute's thrill.

Marian Mack, who plays the role of a Confederate belle, is Buster's new leading lady.

"The General." It was done in the very best tradition of the Northwest. Schedules were changed and Buster's engines allowed to roam at will during the best sunlit hours. At night the regular traffic passed over the tracks.

It was not unusual for passengers along the line to wait patiently for late trains while the Keaton company held up traffic to burn bridges, tear up track and destroy locomotives and cars, all for the entertainment of .... audiences who see "The General."

A Good Feature and Reviews

REVIEW

This is laugh and thrill week at the .... Theatre.

Showing the biggest comedy of all time, "The General," with the famous Buster Keaton as the star, the management's only difficulty is to find enough seats for the crowds.

There are a thousand and one chuckles, roars and gasps in Buster's epic comedy of Civil War days. For his initial feature as a United Artists star, the comedian has turned back the clock three-quarters of a century and brought the lighter chapters of the Civil War to the screen.

Treating the comedy of war days without reverting to slapstick, Keaton manages to keep the action historically accurate as well as unusually mirth-provoking. He proves that battles, railroad wecks, spy plots and war-time love affairs have their laughs.

Buster has built the main plot of "The General" around an actual happening in the struggle between the States. When a band of Northern raiders, disguised as travelers, stole a locomotive and penetrated into Confederate territory, creating havoc and temporarily disrupting the Confederates' military plans, a brave young Southerner started out single-handed to foil them.

The frozen-faced star re-lives the adventures of the sixties and gets into all sorts of predicaments before he finally outwits the Federals, saves his kidnapped sweetheart and wins the plaudits of the populace below the Mason and Dixon line.

"The General" is produced on a massive scale. Thousands of troops are seen in action and real wood-burning Civil War locomotives and trains thunder over the rails. One of the engines in the picture crashes through a burning trestle to furnish the greatest thrill ever filmed. It is a recorded fact that this scene was made at a cost of $40,000 after the crash had been filmed in miniature at an outlay of $1,000.

Joseph M. Schenck, chairman of the board of directors of United Artists and producer of Keaton's pictures, said:

"This scene must be so thrilling that it will bring spectators to their feet. Plunge one of the Civil War locomotives through the burning bridge, no matter how much it costs. Real thrills and laughs in a picture for world-wide distribution are worth anything."

Buster himself directed "The General," and sharing acting honors with him are Marian Mack, his new leading lady, and a cast of noted screen players.

REVIEW

Battles raged on the screen at the .... Theatre yesterday, trains went through burning bridges, Civil War soldiers chased each other with locomotives, hand-cars, horses—and audiences roared with laughter.

It was the opening of Buster Keaton's latest comedy, "The General," a laugh riot, dealing with the lighter chapters of the struggle between the States.

The frozen-faced star has delved into history for his first picture for United Artists and has achieved the biggest success of his career.

Produced on a tremendous scale, "The General" is crammed with mirth and thrills from start to finish.

Minus his pancake hat, Buster, still he of the frozen visage, blossoms forth as a dashing young Southerner who is refused enlistment in the Confederate Army because of his value to the cause as the engineer of "The General," a locomotive.

Spurned by his sweetheart (Marian Mack) and friends because they believe him to be a slacker, Buster finally becomes a hero to the South when he foils, single-handed, a band of Northern adventurers who steal a train, penetrate into Confederate territory and attempt to destroy lines of communication.

The story of "The General" is based upon historical fact—the famous Andrews railroad raid and locomotive chase in Tennessee and Georgia shortly after the outbreak of the Civil War. Real locomotives and trains of the type which thundered over the rails during the sixties play a prominent part in the mirth-provoking production. One of the scenes is the plunge of an engine through a burning bridge, a screen thrill which has never been duplicated.

Buster proves that he is a dramatic star as well as a comedian. He risks life and limb in many of the sensational scenes and makes love like a Don Juan.

Many well-known players appear in the supporting cast. Thousands of soldiers take part in the battles.

Produced by Joseph M. Schenck, "The General" was directed by Keaton himself and Clyde Bruckman.

Good Editors Demand Good Features

COMEDIAN FIRE FIGHTER

Buster Keaton and "The General's" Army Fought Northwest Forest Fire

Stopping work while in the midst of production on his big United Artists comedy spectacle, "The General," which is the feature at the .... Theatre, Buster Keaton and the 600 members of his company and thousands of extras recently helped fight a disastrous forest fire in the Pacific Northwest.

Keaton was on location in Oregon when the timber blazes broke out. His Civil War towns, constructed for the filming of the costliest laugh feature in the history of motion pictures, were believed to be safe from the flames, but Buster, wishing to aid the forest rangers and thousands of volunteers, immediately ceased activities when he heard of the danger and ordered his forces to the edge of forests, which had become veritable infernoes.

The frozen-faced comedian retained his sense of humor even in the face of danger. Clad only in athletic underwear, shoes and a Confederate campaign hat, Buster led his forces to the attack. The heat thawed out his immobile face, and he kept the fire fighters laughing all during the night. The fire became menacing on a Saturday night, and it was then that Buster put the resources of his organization at the command of the Oregon State Officers. The Hollywood contingent stayed on the job until the flames were under control the next day.

Students of history would have received a shock if they could have seen Buster, garbed like a Welsh rarebit dream Marathon runner, leading the Union and Confederate armies against the flames. "The General" is a comedy with a historically accurate Civil War background, and a battle was being fought on the afternoon the fire started. An armistice was decreed until the common enemy was routed.

The hordes of extras, wearers of the blue and the gray, were forced to use the coats of their uniforms as substitutes for blankets to fight the flames.

Motion picture generals and privates, spies and patriots, southern gentlemen and northern adventurers, as well as cameramen, "gag" men, assistant directors, electricians, property men and production officials fought side by side under the leadership of shirtless, pantsless Buster. For several hours the Keaton camps and thousands of acres of virgin forests were believed doomed, but a change in the wind enabled the fighters to check the flames.

The Keaton fire-fighting equipment which was kept in readiness all the time during the several months the company was on location, because of the danger from the three Civil War woodburning locomotives used in the huge comedy, played an important part in getting the forest fire under control.

Several hundred Oregon National Guardsmen, who take part in "The General," also performed heroic service. The Keaton first-aid stations were filled with fire fighters overcome by the smoke, and the wives of the Hollywood group, including Buster's wife, Natalie Talmadge Keaton, a sister of Norma and Constance, prepared sandwiches and coffee for the men.

The frequent forest fires left such a pall of smoke over the entire region that the Keaton company returned to Hollywood by special train, "shot" interiors in "The General" until the fall rains cleared the atmosphere, and then went back to Oregon to complete the picture.

Actual camera work covered a period of more than six months.

Buster leased twelve miles of railroad in Oregon, bought three locomotives and dozens of freight cars and passenger coaches and converted them at great expense into Civil War rolling stock. Bridges and trestles, such as the ones which spanned the rivers in Tennessee and Georgia during the sixties, were built in Oregon. Thousands of dollars were spent for single laughs and thrills.

One of the scenes in "The General" is the plunge of a locomotive through a burning trestle. This action could have been filmed in miniature for less than $1,000, but Joseph M. Schenck, producer of Keaton's pictures, insisted on the real thing, so the wreck was staged at a cost of $40,000.

Those who have seen this scene on the screen declare that it remained for a comedy to furnish the greatest thrill in the history of the silversheet.

"The General" is Buster's first picture for United Artists and is by far the most ambitious comedy in his career.

A Page of News Features

EVER RIDE A HIGH-WHEELED BICYCLE?

Did you ever ride a Civil War bicycle?

Ask grandad, he knows.

Buster Keaton has to master an ancient balky velocipede in "The General," his spectacular comedy of the sixties, at the .... Theatre, but his mirth-provoking antics astride the machine on the silversheet is only half the story.

When the frozen-faced star was filming his first United Artists feature, he spent five days learning to conquer a contrivance that would make the most stubborn flivver of 1926 look like an invalid's wheel chair. Buster took several bad spills before he finally learned the knack of dashing along on the bicycle's granddaddy without breaking his neck.

Keaton uses many means of locomotion in "The General," which is based on the famous Andrews railroad raid and engine chase, a chapter of the Civil War that came near changing history. In his role of a young Confederate fire-eater, Buster pursues the northerners in locomotives, on hand-cars, on horseback and on foot.

He and his sweetheart (Marian Mack) flee over burning bridges and through shell-swept battlefields as the picture unfolds its thousand and one laughs and thrills. A real Civil War locomotive, one of several used in comedy, goes through a blazing trestle to furnish a minute's thrill. This scene alone was made in Oregon at a cost of $40,000 to the Keaton Company.

Thousands of characters appear in "The General," which was produced by Joseph M. Schenck as Buster's initial contribution to the United Artists offering of 1926-7 features.

The uniforms, camps, buildings and quantities of Civil War equipment used in the picture are authentic, experts having spent several months in research work before camera activity started.

Universally hailed as the costliest comedy ever made, "The General" represents a financial outlay exceeded by but few dramatic pictures in the history of the cinema industry.

SUCH IS FAME!

It's great to be famous.

Ask Buster Keaton.

Shortly after the frozen-faced comedy star completed his first United Artists picture, "The General," feature photoplay at the ...., he made a trip back East.

While speeding across the continent Buster planted himself on the observation platform of the limited and was enjoying the scenery when a girl began to eye him suspiciously. As Buster tells it:

"I was wondering whether to give myself up to the authorities when the young lady suddenly inquired, 'Aren't you Buster Keaton?'

"The third degree unnerved me and I confessed.

" 'Will you do me a favor?' she asked.

" 'Yes,' I heroically exclaimed. Anything—absolutely anything but diving off the Washington monument.

" 'Well,' she giggled, 'when you get back to Hollywood, see if you can get an introduction to Constance Talmadge and ask for a picture of herself for me.' "

THEY LET HIM LIVE

"The General" is the title of Buster Keaton's first United Artists picture under the Joseph M. Schenck banner, which comes to the....................Theatre .... And "The General" is a locomotive, one of several used in the Civil War comedy, and not a military officer.

During the filming of the spectacular comedy, which utilizes the services of several thousand people and unfolds some of the lighter but most thrilling chapters of the struggle between the States, a studio wit approached Buster and asked the frozen-faced star if he knew that his engine chewed tobacco.

"Yes, sir, 'The General' chews tobacco."

"How do you figure that?" asked Keaton.

"Well, it choo choos to start 'er, and it choo choos to back 'er."

$1,000,000 COMEDIES COMING

Buster Keaton, Who Spent $500,000 on His Own, "The General," Foresees Higher Cost of Laugh Production
By BUSTER KEATON

The day of the million dollar motion picture *comedy* is not far distant.

People would rather laugh than weep, and if they have to pay for the privilege of doing either, it is obvious which form of entertainment they'll choose. That's why I've never had a secret desire to play Hamlet or star in dramatic "epics."

As an illustration of the staggering cost and months of effort required to make a feature comedy of the type demanded by the world's screen fans, I might give a few facts in connection with "The General," which was produced by Joseph M. Schenck as my first picture for United Artists.

Nearly a year ago our organization began searching for material for a comedy with a Civil War background—a picture that would combine laughs with thrills but still not burlesque any phase of the struggle between the States. We finally hit upon a certain chapter of the war as a basis for the story. It was the historic Andrews railroad raid and locomotive chase.

Students of history and Civil War survivors will recall the feat of a band of daring Northerners who penetrated into Confederate territory, stole a locomotive and part of a train, played general havoc with military plans and who subsequently were chased, and many of them captured, by the boys in gray.

It wasn't very funny to anyone concerned at the time, but as we look back, the adventure was replete with comedy. We pledged ourselves to make every phase of the picture historically accurate and not to take liberties with even the smallest episode.

It was our original plan to film the picture in Tennessee, the locale of the chief part of the story. Location scouts spent several weeks in the south and east, searching for a region resembling the railroad raid territory of the sixties. Alas for the progress of the south! We didn't find what we wanted. We had to have several miles of railroad track and have it for our almost exclusive use during the making of "The General." The south's railroads of today were too busy and too modern for our purposes.

After traveling nearly 14,000 miles, I found in Oregon a location which research workers took oath is more like the Tennessee of the sixties than Tennessee was itself. A mountainous country where we could have a railroad practically to ourselves for several months, and nobody to bother us when we staged Civil War battles, ran locomotives into rivers, burned and blew up bridges and generals enjoyed a Hollywood holiday.

Our troubles started when we got ready to leave Hollywood for Oregon. We bought three old locomotives and many freight cars and passenger coaches and had them rebuilt into rolling stock of the Civil War period. We had planned to run them under their own power up the coast, but as they didn't boast any airbrakes, the railroad said, "No." So the engines and trains went on flatcars.

When we arrived in Oregon we had to build towns, hire thousands of extras to enact the roles of Federal and Confederate soldiers—and incidentally provide the correct uniforms for them—set up commissary camps, hospitals, blacksmith shops, isolated storehouses for the huge quantities of powder used in the battle scenes, employ fire wardens to protect the forests from damage, and even engage teachers to school the many children on location.

Thousands of spectators came from miles around to watch us film "The General." On the day that we plunged one of our three locomotives from a burning trestle into the river below and spent $40,000 for a single screen thrill, half of the state of Oregon must have been there to see the scene "shot."

One of the big laughs in connection with our location trip was at the expense of the barber in a town where we made our headquarters for several weeks. When he heard that a Hollywood motion picture company was coming, he added several chairs and hired some extra barbers. But we were all Civil War types and had sworn off hair-cuts until the picture was completed. And most of the company wore beards which didn't require any trimming.

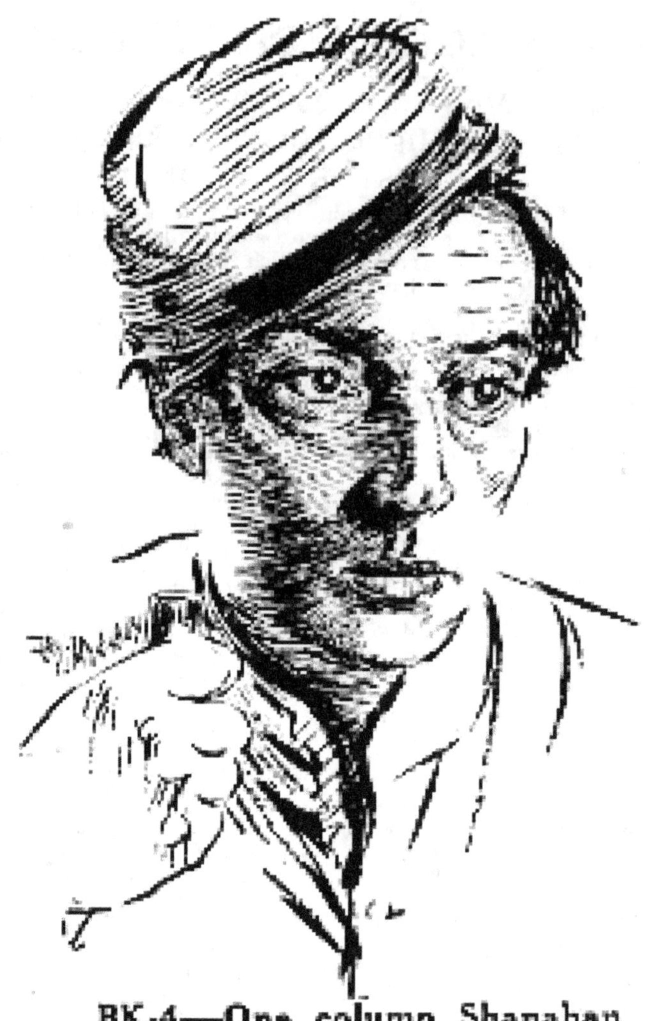

BK-4—One column Shanahan
sketch. Mat only 5c

Buster Keaton, "frozen-faced" star of "The General" at the............................ Theatre, recently saw Helen Wills, the American tennis star—"little Miss Poker Face"—play tennis. When Greek meets Greek!

John Barrymore recently bet Buster Keaton, star of "The General," a box of cigars he could tell a funny story that would make Buster smile. John told it. Buster remained his frozen-faced self. Then Barrymore handed over the cigars. Buster lit one, puffed delightedly and beamed a smile of contentment. And Barrymore took back the cigars!

The barber got one look at the Hollywood visitors, whom he expected to be at least daily customers, and promptly fired his extra help and took out the rush-season chairs.

"The General," Buster Keaton's first independent film for United Artists, took twice as long to make and cost twice as much money as any previous Keaton comedy. So Buster calls it "a comedy spectacle."

A Page of News Features

ACTOR IN KEATON FILM REMEMBERS '65

Frederick Vroom, who portrays a Confederate military leader in "The General," produced by Joseph M. Schenck as Buster Keaton's first United Artists picture, at the............................... Theatre, had a notable stage career before he cast his lot with motion pictures.

Born in Nova Scotia 69 years ago, Mr. Vroom remembers vividly the shock his family received at the news of Lincoln's assassination. He moved to Massachusetts as a boy and was visiting in Philadelphia when he attended a theatre for the first time. The youth had to be coaxed by the friends whom he was visiting to go with them to the theatre. He had refused the invitations several times, but when Edwin Booth came to play a two-week engagement at the old Walnut Street Theatre, the temptation was too much to withstand.

The incident changed the motive of the boy's life entirely. He began immediately to read Shakespeare and study for the stage. In the spring of 1884 he had graduated from the Lyceum Theatre School of Dramatic Arts— afterwards known as the American Academy of Dramatic Art.

Young Vroom had a small part in "Dakolar" and "The Iron Master" at the opening of the New Lyceum Theatre, Robert Mantell, John Mason and Sadie Martinot were in the cast. That was in May of 1884.

Afterwards he played with Modjeska, Thomas Keene and others until 1900, when he left the stage to go to Alaska during the rush to Nome and did not return to the stage until 1910.

Mr. Vroom won instant success when he entered motion pictures several years ago, and has since played in many important productions, climaxing his career with his work in "The General."

KEATON KNOCKED DOWN BY EXPLOSION IN FILM

Some of the big scenes in "The General," the new Buster Keaton comedy which comes to the........................Theatre ...., nearly ended in tragedy when the picture was being made.

Audiences do not know that men are fighting desperately for their lives as some of the action in the big comedy is flashing across the silversheet. One of these scenes is the attempt of the Northern raiders in the Civil War story to swim a rapids to escape their Confederate pursuers.

On the day that this scene was made on the McKenzie River in Oregon, Buster, as his own director, kept the cameras grinding as long as possible, then plunged into the rapids himself and saved two of the supporting players from drowning.

The rapids through which the actors swam are so rough that boats are not permitted to descend them. A battery of cameras had been placed on rocks in mid-stream, and during the height of the "shooting" one of them fell into the raging torrent and was demolished.

The scene is considered one of the most dangerous ever attempted, both from the standpoint of the actors and the camera men.

Another scene that kept the Keaton first-aid stations busy on the day it was made was the blowing up of a dam by Buster while the raiders were under heavy Confederate fire. The dam blew up with a vengeance, showering members of the company with rock and requiring stitches in several heads.

Buster was thrown down by the force of the explosion, but he kept his wits and his frozen-face, and indicated to the cameraman that he wanted the action to continue till the end of the scene.

Minor casualties were frequent during the filming of "The General," which took six months to make. The cast numbers thousands. The equipment in the picture includes three Civil War locomotives and trains, historically accurate in every detail.

Produced by Joseph M. Schenck, "The General" is Keaton's first United Artists picture and is the costliest comedy ever made.

A Page of News Features

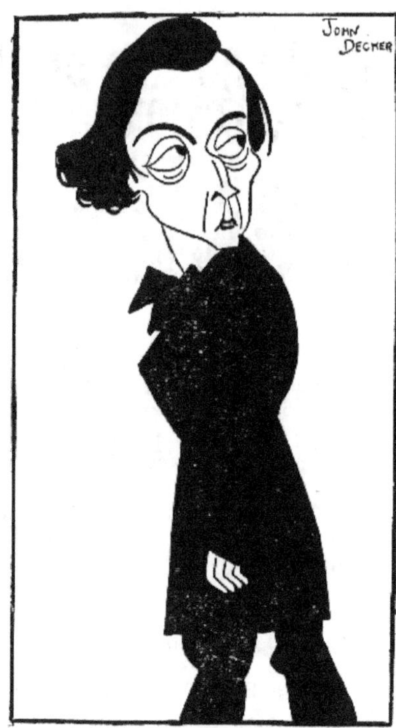

**BK-3—Decker Sketches
4 on Mat 10c**

STAR OF "THE GENERAL" CAME FROM KANSAS

Buster Keaton, star and director of "The General," the feature at the .... "................ Theatre, was born on November 4, 1895, at Pickway, Kansas, where Buster's father, Joe Keaton, then in partnership with Harry Houdini, was filling a tent show engagement.

When the elder Keaton and Houdini dissolved partnership, Buster's father and mother, Myra Keaton, formed a vaudeville act and Buster joined it at the age of three. From that time till 1916, when Buster entered pictures, the three Keatons toured America and many foreign countries.

Buster went to France as a private in 1917 and, returning to Hollywood after the armistice, resumed his affiliation with the Joseph M. Schenck organization. After starring in two-reel comedies, Buster entered the feature field.

Some of Buster's famous comedies are "Three Ages," "Hospitality," "Sherlock Junior," "The Navigator," "Seven Chances," "Go West" and "Battling Butler."

"The General," a historical comedy spectacle, is his first feature for the United Artists. He directs his own starring vehicle.

KEATON FILM BASED ON HISTORICAL FACT

"The General," Buster Keaton's latest comedy, and the feature attraction next week at the .... Theatre, has an authentic Civil War background, being based on one of the most thrilling chapters of the struggle between the States—the famous Andrews railroad raid and locomotive chase.

Andrews and a score of Union men captured the locomotive, "The General," at Big Shanty, Georgia, in April, 1862, hoping to make their way to Chattanooga, burning bridges and destroying the road on their way, thus preventing the Southern army from succoring Chattanooga. The success of this raid might have turned the tide of the war.

Buster plays the part of the engineer on "The General." He is refused admission into the Southern army, although his sweetheart has informed him that unless he puts on the gray of the South she will have nothing further to do with him. The reason for the refusal of h's enlistment is that the military authorities believe him to be of more value to the cause as an engineer.

His friends of the South turn against him, thinking it merely a subterfuge to avoid service. His girl turns him down. His only friend is his locomotive.

So, when the Andrews raiders steal it, he starts in pursuit, not so much to do his duty to the cause as to rescue his only friend and companion, "The General." He follows the raiders so closely that they are prevented from carrying through their bridge burning plans. However, he follows them too closely, and finds himself within the Northern lines, where he is captured.

His sweetheart, who was on the train, is likewise made a captive inadvertently, as she was in the baggage car looking through her trunk when the raid started. She thinks Buster's appearance on the scene is to rescue her. Buster manages to escape with the girl, seize "The General" and starts back. He has learned of plans for an attack on the South which he unconsciously manages to frustrate by accidently blocking the way, and giving warning. He is acclaimed a hero and is permitted to enlist, his sweetheart forgiving him, and the friends who shunned him idolizing him. He is likewise appointed a lieutenant in the Southern Army.

"The General" was produced on a lavish scale, with thousands in the supporting cast, and the use of miles of specially built railroad.

A Page of News Features

BUSTER KEATON TUMBLED TO FAME

"How does Buster Keaton keep from breaking his neck, or his arms and legs, when he makes those funny falls in his pictures?"

That's a question which puzzles millions of movie fans who are being thrilled by his first United Artists Picture, "The General," at the...................... Theatre.

For years the frozen-faced star has been convulsing and thrilling the public with acrobatic stunts which would land the ordinary mortal in the hospital —or the morgue. The secret of his ability to suddenly stub his toe and fall on his face, or tumble down a flight of stairs without injuring himself, is simple: a lifetime of training and constant practice, plus a physique envied by many professional athletes.

Buster Keaton has tumbled and slam-banged his way through life. He started his mirth-provoking acrobatics when he was a baby. As most film fans know, the stork arrived with Buster during a Kansas cyclone. The future star's father and Harry Houdini, world-famous as an escape king and magician, were partners in a tent show. The troupe was touring the Middle West, and on the night that the baby was born the tent vanished during the height of the twister. Buster's mother was carried into a church, and it was there the big event took place.

The boy's arrival failed to interfere with the tour. Buster—his name was Joseph at the start—became a trouper from the day of his birth and has been entertaining the public ever since, with the exception of eighteen months spent in the A. E. F. during the World War.

Young Keaton began practicing his trick falls at the age of six months. One day, in a hotel, the tot fell all the way downstairs, and seemed to enjoy the experience.

"What a buster!" exclaimed Houdini, and the name stuck.

A few years later the elder Keaton and Houdini dissolved partnership, and father, mother and Buster became the Three Keatons, who for many years were vaudeville headliners all over America and abroad. Theatregoers will remember how Joe Keaton used to pick little Buster up, as if he were a bag of meal, and hurl the boy around the stage, knocking down scenery and bringing gasps from the audience. In several cities, children's soceities complained to the authorities that Buster was being mistreated; once the boy was called before the Governor of New York and stripped to prove he didn't have any bruises or broken bones.

Buster got as much enjoyment out of diving on his ear and letting his dad use him for a human medicine ball as most American boys do in playing shinny and run-sheep-run. The future movie star would spend hours perfecting falls which didn't hurt him, but which looked like real accidents.

By the time he was twenty years old, Buster was regarded as one of the greatest stage acrobats, as well as comedians. But he never stopped practising, and when he entered pictures, his prowess as an acrobat played a big part in winning him early fame on the screen.

Advance Or During Run

KEATON'S RAILROAD COMEDY COMING

Unrivaled dramatic thrills—
Spectacular battle scenes—
The greatest railroad crash ever filmed—

A blood-tingling love story—
And the most laughs ever crammed into a motion picture.

That, in a nutshell, is "The General," Buster Keaton's colossal comedy, which is playing to packed houses at the ....Theatre.

Produced on a lavish scale by Joseph M. Schenck, chairman of the board of directors of United Artists, as the frozen-faced star's first feature for United Artists, "The General" is at once the costliest and most ambitious laugh picture in the history of the screen.

The story is built around certain of the lighter chapters of the Civil War and is enacted on the silversheet with every degree of historical accuracy. Keaton has taken a stirring page from the sixties—the famous Andrews railroad raid and locomotive chase—and made it into several thousand feet of record-breaking celluloid entertainment.

Thousands of people appear in the big photoplay, which required more than six months to produce.

Several locomotives and scores of railroad cars were bought outright by the Keaton organization and converted into Civil War period equipment; museums of the country were combed for battle relics; a number of towns were built as replicas of the Tennessee and Georgia communities which figure in the story; entire companies and troops of the national guard were recruited to serve as Union and Confederate soldiers.

Buster, who also directed "The General," has the mirth-provoking role of a young Southern patriot who blunders his way into fame and the affections of *the* girl when a band of Federal raiders swoop down upon the Confederates, steal a train and play havoc with the South's military plans. The frozen-faced farceur pilots the wood-burning engines, figures in wrecks, helps the generals win their battles and finally convinces the Confederates he is a hero instead of a slacker.

Marian Mack, a young actress who deserted starring roles in dramatic features for the opportunity to play opposite Keaton in the biggest comedy ever made, portrays a Southern belle and the star's companion during his ludicrous adventures.

"The General." It was done in the very best tradition of the Northwest. Schedules were changed and Buster's engines allowed to roam at will during the best sunlit hours. At night the regular traffic passed over the tracks.

It was not unusual for passengers along the line to wait patiently for late trains while the Keaton company held up traffic to burn bridges, tear up track and destroy locomotives and cars, all for the entertainment of .... audiences who see "The General."

"POWDER MAN" HAS NO EASY JOB ON KEATON FILM

His name is Jack Little. But his job is a big one. He looks after the powder during filming of pictures. When Buster Keaton wanted somebody to take care of all the dynamite and powder to be used in "The General," his comedy spectacle at the .... Theatre, he found Little.

Fifteen years ago the unusual "powder man" got interested in pictures. He has been injured four times and he was nearly blown to the heaven of all good picture folk during the filming of "The General" in Oregon. When the soldiers were trooping across the fields in "The Big Parade," Little kept the powder under surveillance. Naturally, therefore Buster picked the same powder man to do the honors for the ammunition employed by the Southerners and Northerners in the Keaton film.

These Southerners and Northerners, by the way, battled all day long and then drew pay checks from the same paymaster, ate in the same mess hall and talked about the same favorite

comedian. The people of Cottage Grove, Oregon, where much of "The General" was made, shared the enthusiasm of the "warriors" for Buster, since Cottage Grove was one of the first towns in America to exhibit "The General" in film form.

After Your Opening

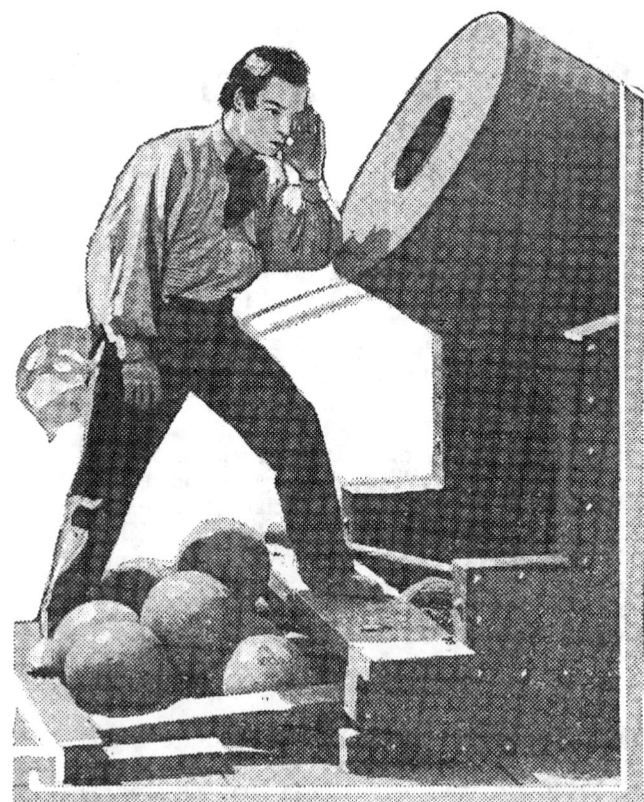

BK-7—Two Col. Scene Cut 50c. Mat 10c

"WHAT A BUSTER"

Buster Keaton, whose new comedy spectacle, "The General," is at the .... Theatre, was born on November 4, 1895, in Pickway, Kansas. A few months later a cyclone blew Pickway off the map. And it's still off.

For many years Buster's father, Joe Keaton, was in partnership with Harry Houdini, afterward the famous magician. Houdini and the senior Keaton had a tent show. When Buster was six months old he fell downstairs.

"What a buster!" said Houdini when he found that young Keaton wasn't hurt.

"That's a good name for the kid," declared Buster's father. And "Buster" it has been ever since.

CLEARED THE TRACK FOR "THE GENERAL"

They cleared the track for "The General" up in Oregon, where Buster Keaton's puffing iron horse chugged its way to a cinematic triumph, as visitors to the .... Theatre this week will testify. Railroads in the Pacific Northwest are nothing if not accommodating, so they changed schedules on a branch line for three months in order to let "The General" charge along a twelve-mile stretch of track all by itself.

When Buster had chosen the rough country in the vicinity of Cottage Grove, Oregon, as the district which today most resembles the railroad country of Tennessee and Georgia in the sixties, it became necessary for some railroad to set aside certain tracks then in use for the exclusive travels of "The General." It was done in the very best tradition of the Northwest. Schedules were changed and Buster's engines allowed to roam at will during the best sunlit hours. At night the regular traffic passed over the tracks.

It was not unusual for passengers along the line to wait patiently for late trains while the Keaton company held up traffic to burn bridges, tear up track and destroy locomotives and cars, all for the entertainment of .... audiences who see "The General."

PRIVATE IN SPANISH WAR: GENERAL ON SCREEN

One of the interesting personalities in Buster Keaton's supporting cast in "The General," the frozen-faced comedy star's first picture for United Artists and the costliest laugh feature ever made under the Joseph M. Schenck banner, is James Farley.

Farley, a veteran of the silver sheet, has the role of a Northern General in he spectacular Civil War comedy at he ....Theatre.

Born at Waldron, Arkansas, on January 8, 1883, Farley went on the stage at the age of twelve. A few years later, yearning for adventure, he joined the United States army in time to fight in the Philippine rebellion.

Farley left the service in 1901 and took a position in the United States Treasury Department.

He played in his first motion picture in 1912 and since then has enacted hundreds of roles in films.

Newspapers Like Biographies

DEAF—BUT HEARD DINNER BELL

By BUSTER KEATON
(Star of "The General at the . . . . Theatre)

" 'Twas a long way to Tipperary for the Tommies during the late unpleasantness, but a darn sight longer way back to Hollywood for a certain Yank.

How he foiled the European chapter of the Amalgamated Order of Conquering Cooties and got back to the land of Moonlight and Roses—and Cafeterias—proves that turning points in careers are like hairpin turns— you have to slow down while making 'em.

Came the day—as the title writers don't say any more—when an actor whom we will refer to in these confessions as "Frozen-Face," landed in New York after an engagement abroad, said engagement officially terminating in November, 1918, on the occasion of Young Peace Dove knocking Kid Mars for a loop. But, on account of traffic jams on the Atlantic Ocean and other unavoidable delays, the foreign time act ran unofficially until 1919.

The early months of that year found Frozen-Face doing a stretch on a cot in a New York hospital—taking the rest cure, as it were, and renewing acquaintance with white sheets. The worst part of the whole deal was that he couldn't hear—not even the dinner bell, which was particularly tough.

Hollywood then seemed as far away as the South Pole. Frozen-Face had left the Kleig Light Capital in 1917. He was playing in two-reel comedies when he exchanged his pancake hat for a style of chapeau that suddenly became extremely popular all over the United States. The only way you could acquire one of the aforesaid bonnets was to learn the combination of a piece of tinware called a mess kit. This entitled you to the pass-word, "Come and get it."

Anyway, on a certain day in 1919, Frozen-Face was reclining on his downy couch, reading something—it either was "The History of the Honey Bee," or "The Battles of John L. Sullivan," the actor forgets which, and listening to the woodpeckers at work on a nearby building. As a matter of fact, steel riveters were doing their stuff on a New York skyscraper, but they sounded like woodpeckers to Frozen-Face.

A visitor was announced. Our subject didn't hear any announcement; sounds nicer, though, to always speak of them as being announced.

It was Joe Schenck—Joseph M. Schenck. Now, Mr. Schenck was the man behind the pictures in which Frozen-Face had appeared. The producer talked, and Frozen-Face nodded his head and said "Sure" and "Certainly"— just as if he knew what Mr. Schenck was talking about.

Finally Frozen-Face, fearing that his boss would think he was conversing with a goofy individual, asked Mr. Schenck to write it out.

The producer did, and he said, in effect, that Frozen-Face had a job waiting for him in Hollywood, and was going to get the chance to be a full-fledged comedy star.

Talk about the thrill that comes once in a lifetime? That was Frozen-Face's. "California, Here I Come," hadn't been written yet, but if it had, the woodpeckers would have been playing it!

That was the turning point in B. K.'s career.

The woodpeckers don't peck any more—at least, they're real birds, not steel workers, if they do. And the perpetrator of this sketch can now hear any kind of a dinner bell perfectly.

Newspapers Like Biographies

BUSTER'S LEADING LADY SMALL TOWN GIRL

Marian Mack, a dashing little brunette, plays opposite Buster Keaton in "The General," the costliest comedy spectacle in the history of pictures, and the frozen-faced star's first feature for United Artists, at the.................Theatre.

Miss Mack's work in "The General" has been hailed by critics as a revelation, as it was not long ago that the little leading lady was a motion picture bathing beauty. In the Keaton comedy, which has an authentic and historically accurate background, Marian proves that she is a real actress and one worthy of stardom. In her role of a Southern belle of crinoline days and the idol of the Confederate soldiers, she shines both as a comedienne and as a dramatic actress.

Yes, Marian is Buster's sweetheart in "The General," and chief cause of most of his adventures. Keaton, portraying a young Confederate patriot who is refused for service in the army because of his value to the cause as a locomotive engineer, goes through all kinds of laughable and thrilling adventures to prove to his sweetheart and her family that he is not a slacker.

Miss Mack is modest. On the set or in her various social activities, she has a good word for everyone. She has none of what writers are pleased to term temperament.

Miss Mack is proud of the fact that she came from a small town. It was about three years ago that a little Eureka, Utah, schoolgirl dreamed the dream of millions of other girls in all parts of the world. But she did more than dream; she told herself that she *could* make good in Hollywood if she had the opportunity, and she determined to create the opportunity. She wrote a letter to one of the world's foremost producers of comedies, explaining her ambitions. Fate must have been in league with the girl, for something happened that happens very seldom in real or reel life. She received a reply from the producer, inviting her and her mother to come to Hollywood for an interview. She came, and saw, and conquered. And within a few months she was playing featured roles in two-reel comedies. But a two-reel comedienne and bathing beauty was not her goal. Then, as now, she preferred comedy to anything else and she had her eyes on the feature field, so when the opportunity came to appear in longer pictures she made good with a vengeance.

Everyone was talking about her cameo-like beauty and acting ability when Keaton launched plans for his most ambitious picture. He chose Miss Mack from among a score of feminine stars and leading ladies, practically all of them of much wider experience than the former Utah girl.

Perhaps because she is a "small town" girl Miss Mack prefers home life to anything else, even in Hollywood. When the work at the studio is over for the day she finds her recreation in her artistic Spanish style residence in the hills overlooking the motion picture capital. She is a great reader and an accomplished musician.

Others may have their golf and tennis and swimming and horseback riding to keep in condition, but Miss Mack's favorite exercise is bicycle riding. Although she is an all-round sportswoman she peddles her way to physical fitness along secluded paths in the vicinity of her home.

After Your Opening

What? No Austrians?

"Buster Keaton—Austrian."

A press dispatch from Europe announcing that this designation of a nationality had been wished upon the frozen-faced comedian by some newspapers, elicited the following reply from at the .... Theatre, and Buster's first United Artists Picture.

"If I'm an Austrian, Norma and Constance Talmadge must be the Siamese Twins, Charley Chaplin a Hottentot and Harry Lauder a spendthrift."

> The general opinion about "The General" is that Buster Keaton has scored a tremendous hit. Your private opinion of "The General" will be the same!

Newspapers Like Biographies

COMEDIAN MUST BE "FROZEN-FACE" ALWAYS

Buster Keaton's life has been a solemn one.

All his life the star of "The General," the Civil War laugh feature at the.........................Theatre, has been making others laugh, yet he is never granted for his own part a levity lighter than an undertaker heading a procession. As if that were not enough, he can never show any real grief.

Buildings may tumble upon his head, trains run off the track and locomotives plunge into rivers, as in "The General." Animals may sample his anatomy and horses step on his face, yet he is always prohibited from expressing the pain he feels.

Buster the "frozen-faced" he was dubbed, and Buster the "frozen-faced" he has to be.

The famous comedy star's latest picture is his first for United Artists. It is based on the famous Andrews railroad raid and locomotive chase, one of the most thrilling chapters of the Civil War, and it combines historical accuracy with hilarious situations.

The big comedy, produced by Joseph M. Schenck and directed by Keaton himself, is the costliest screen opus of its kind ever made. Months were spent in filming "The General," and the company of thousands traveled to distant parts of the United States in their search for locations. Civil War towns were reconstructed, miles of railroad leased and three locomotives and dozens of freight cars and passenger coaches purchased and converted into old rolling stock.

BUSTER PICKED MARIAN IN A THEATRE

Buster Keaton has a system all his own in selecting a leading lady.

That's why Marian Mack, who was comparatively unknown in Hollywood until about a year ago, has the feminine lead in "The General," the frozen-faced star's first picture for United Artists, and the feature comedy at the .... Theatre this week.

Several months before Keaton, whose pictures are all produced by Joseph M. Schenck, decided to make an elaborate comedy with a Civil War background, he began scouting for a girl who was his idea of a Confederate belle during the sixties. He didn't care whether his leading lady in "The General" had been in pictures six years or six months —or whether, so long as she had ability, she had ever appeared before the camera. Buster wanted a girl with the charm and poise of the old South, a beauty such as the average individual imagines his grandmother was as a maid.

So Keaton searched and searched and was almost in despair until one night he saw a girl walk down the aisle of a Los Angeles theatre in which he and Mrs. Keaton were enjoying a musical show.

"There's the girl to play in 'The General' if she can act and wants the job," exclaimed Buster.

An introduction was arranged, screen tests made the following day, and within twenty-four hours a contract had been signed.

"THE GENERAL COMMANDS LAUGHS

"The General" is in town!

It's the big laugh spectacle which is convulsing audiences at the.....................Theatre.

Based on the humorous side of the Civil War and with Buster Keaton as the star, "The General" represents the last word in elaborate comedies. The picture was produced on such a vast scale that it took nearly a year to make and necessitated a financial outlay which would be sufficient for all but a few of the biggest dramatic productions of the past few years.

The story deals with the feat of a band of Northerners who stole a train and raided Confederate territory during the early part of the Civil War. They tore up track, destroyed telegraphic communication and would have disrupted the South's military plans had it not been for a young Confederate locomotive engineer who chased them single-handed and finally caused their capture.

This foolhardy lad comes to life on the screen in the person of Buster Keaton. He and his frozen-face get laughs out of the most dangerous situations and take part in crucial battles as if they were pink teas.

Thrills crowd laughs for honors in many of the scenes in "The General." One of the three authentic Civil War engines which figure in the comedy is run onto a high, burning trestle and plunged into the river below, completely wrecking it.

The railroad chase, in which Buster and his sweetheart (Marian Mack) pursue the train stealers and in turn are chased by them, is said to have brought cheers from audiences in many of the larger cities where "The General" has been shown.

Keaton has a supporting cast of thousands.

"The General" is the famous star's first United Artists Picture and was produced by Joseph M. Schenck.

Advance Or During Run

GREAT STONE FACE

When Buster Keaton and members of his technical staff were touring the Southern States in their quest for historical data in connection with "The General," his big comedy spectacle of the Civil War, which is now at the.................. Theatre, the party visited the famous Stone Mountain.

They were gazing at the Great Stone Face, carved by nature on the bluff.

A schoolchild, an admirer of the frozen-faced comedian, recognized her hero, and within a few minutes Buster was surrounded by a bevy of youngsters who had been picnicking nearby.

The little girl grouped her friends around Buster and addressed them thusly:

"This is Buster Keaton, kids, and he's the Great Stone Face whose pitcher is on the mountain. Ain't I right, Mr. Keaton?"

"Sure," replied Buster. "Now let's go and get some ice cream cones as your reward for. getting my face on such a big mountain. I have two boys about your age and I want to bring them down here some day and show them my picture in stone."

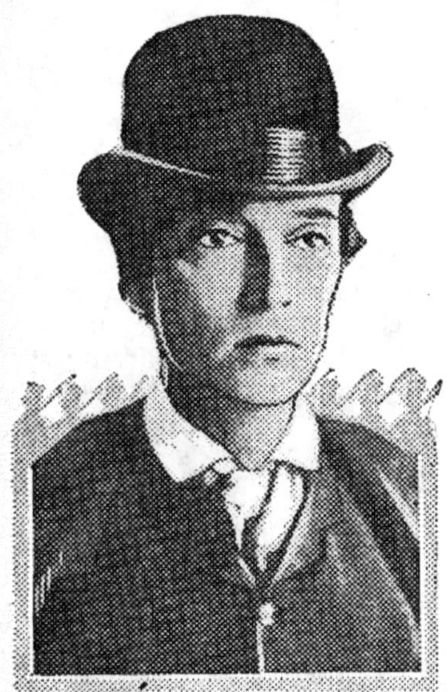

BK-6—One Col. Scene
Cut 30c; Mat 5c

THREE THOUSAND PEOPLE IN BUSTER KEATON COMEDY

In producing "The General," the first big Buster Keaton picture for United Artists, at the.......................Theatre this week, Joseph M. Schenck provided the frozen-faced star with the largest company and the costliest settings and equipment ever assembled for a comedy.

As many as three thousand people were on the payroll during the filming of the Civil War laugh feature, a picture which treats of the lighter side of the war between the states but which does not in any way burlesque the stirring events of the sixties.

"The General" was in production for more than six months, the Keaton company being forced to travel thousands of miles from Hollywood to find the right locations. At one location in Oregon, where six cameras were used to "shoot" some of the biggest scenes, Buster and his army of actors and technical workers spent ten weeks. Three locomotives and scores of freight cars and passengers, rebuilt into Civil War period rolling stock, were taken to Oregon from Hollywood and twelve miles of railroad track leased.

Civil War towns were erected along the right of way, modern bridges dismantled and wooden trestles, such as were in use along the Atlantic & Western line in Tennessee and Georgia in the sixties, substituted.

Because of the danger from forest fires caused by sparks from the old wood-burning locomotives which figure in "The General," special arrangements were made with the state of Oregon to have a small army of fire wardens on duty constantly. Physicians and nurses were on hand all during the filming of the picture to care for the casualties in the battle scenes and the spectacular railway wrecks.

"The General" is based on the historic Andrews railroad raid during the war, when a band of northerners stole an engine and penetrated into Confederate territory, tearing up track, destroying telegraph wires and burning bridges as they headed for Chattanooga.

Keaton, who directed "The General" with Clyde Bruckman, is supported by a big cast of well known principals and thousands of extras.

Marian Mack is Buster's leading lady in the spectacular Civil War comedy.

Good Ones Before Opening

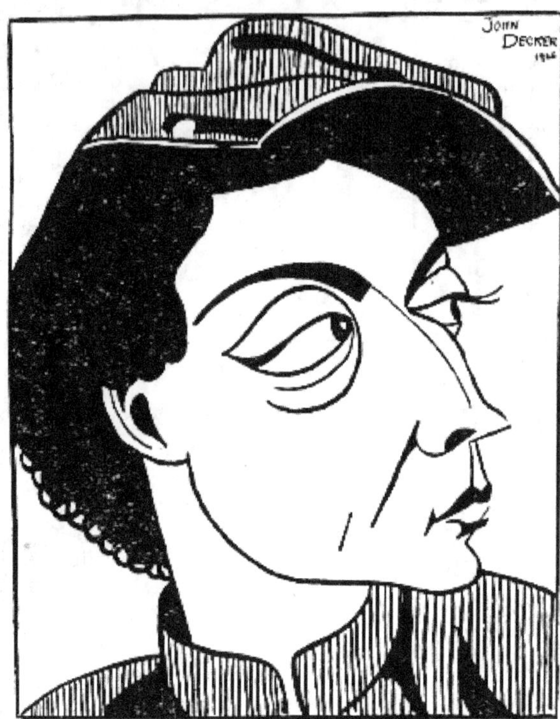

**BK-3—One Col. Sketches
4 on Mat 10c**

IF I HAD A VACATION

By BUSTER KEATON

(Star of "The General at the . . . . Theatre)

I'm not going to get a week's vacation—not the kind of a vacation I mean—so this will be a pipe dream. Vacations are the bunk, anyway.

It takes me a month to prepare for a week's vacation, and a month to rest up after one. Therefore I must have nine weeks—and my wife and children, office boy, cameramen, "gag" men, police dogs and sparring partners say it can't be done without a permit from a congressional investigating committee.

But if the millennium arrived and I found myself with a week's loafing at my disposal, I'd:

Start hunting for the bird who first said, "So's Your Old Man." After gleefully slaying him I'd:

Run amuck until no wise crackers were left to thank you for the buggy ride, and then:

Try to find a Russian refugee who held lower rank than general before the revolution, and if I had any time left:

Take in a few baseball games and boxing bouts, go to a circus, if there were one in town; ride the roller coaster at the beach, eat hot dogs, peanuts and popcorn until I couldn't hold any more,—

And then go home and sleep until Monday morning rolled around again.

Good Ones Before Opening

KEATON WORKED SIX MONTHS BEFORE FILMING ONE SCENE

Months of preparation elapsed before a single scene was made in "The General," Buster Keaton's first United Artists Picture which comes to the ....Theatre................, after being hailed by critics who have seen it as the most elaborate comedy spectacle in the history of the motion picture industry.

Technical and research workers traveled thousands of miles through the east and south in their quest for data in connection with the Civil War story. Thousands of uniforms had to be specially tailored, great quantities of old rifles, pistols, swords, artillery pieces and other relics assembled and tons of properties and acres of sets built.

One of the unique features was the purchase of three old locomotives and scores of freight cars and passenger coaches and their reconstruction into railroad rolling stock of the sixties.

All this mass of material, destined to play an important part in producing the big laugh feature based on the historic Andrews railroad raid and locomotive chase in Tennessee and Georgia, was transported by special train to Oregon, where the Keaton company spent several months on location.

The spectacle of thousands of actors, garbed as Union and Confederate soldiers, engaged in battle, burning bridges, blowing up trains and dotting the countryside with their war-like camps, attracted throngs to the Keaton location from all parts of the Pacific coast. It was estimated that there were 12,000 people on hand the day Keaton spent $40,000 on a scene that occupies a minute's time on the screen — the plunge of a real locomotive from a burning trestle into the river below.

After completing the spectacular scenes on location, Keaton and his "General" company returned to Hollywood and spent several weeks filming interiors at the frozen-faced star's big studio. Many more weeks were required to edit and cut the mass of film.

"The General," which was produced under the Joseph M. Schenck banner, is Keaton's first United Artists Picture. Directed by Buster himself and Clyde Bruckman, the historically accurate Civil War comedy boasts a notable supporting cast, including Marian Mack, the star's new leading lady.

"THE GENERAL" MADE SPECTATORS HYSTERICAL

Realism in motion pictures:

When spectators, watching a scene being "shot," become hysterical.

This actually happened while Buster Keaton was making his latest picture, "The General," at the..................Theatre. And it's a comedy, too; in fact, the biggest comedy in the history of the cinema industry, costing more to make and taking longer to produce than any previous laugh feature.

One scene alone represents an expenditure of $40,000, and it represents less than a minute's action on the screen. It is the crash of a real locomotive through a burning trestle into a river hundreds of feet below, and on the day that the wreck was filmed, thousands of spectators were on hand to see the thrill enacted.

When the Civil War type railway engine, one of the three especially built for "The General," fell through the blazing bridge and plunged into the stream with an explosion that could be heard over a radius of several miles in Oregon, where the Keaton Company was on location, it was the signal for thousands of Union soldiers to ford the river and pursue the Confederates.

The excitement of witnessing a real railroad wreck in such a spectacular setting, followed by the sight of great masses of troops milling around in the water, with numbers of soldiers swimming for their lives after being thrown from their horses, was too much for many of the women in the great audience. Screams from the spectators could be heard above the din.

Seemingly the only calm persons among the thousands were Buster himself, directing his own picture, and the dozen cinematographers behind the battery of cameras that recorded the $40,000 thrill.

The doctors who were on hand to care for casualties in the battle scenes were forced to devote some of their time to hysterical spectators.

Produced by Joseph M. Schenck, "The General" is Buster's first United Artists picture.

General Advance Stories

HISTORICAL ACCURACY IN KEATON PICTURE

Historical accuracy was insisted upon by Joseph M. Schenck, producer of Buster Keaton's pictures, when the frozen-faced comedian decided to make "The General," Civil War comedy spectacle, which comes to the............................ Theatre..............................

The picture is concerned with the lighter side of the famous Andrews railroad raid in April, 1862, when a score of Union daredevils captured a locomotive at Big Shanty, Ga. The comedy, Keaton himself says, is in no sense a burlesque of the Civil War or of any incident thereof.

Buster and his staff of technical aides made extensive trips to New York, Georgia, Tennessee and actual Civil War battle sites, occupying several months with research and collection of historical data. Thousands of extras were garbed as Confederate and Union soldiers during the filming of "The General."

Keaton himself directed the picture, in which he plays the part of the son of the South who is so loyal to his homeland and so unconsciously brilliant as a military strategist that he blocks the progress of the Northern forces singlehandedly.

A study of history reveals the fact that in April of 1862, when the Andrews railroad raid took place at Big Shanty, Ga., a group of Union bravealls captured "The General," which was a locomotive and not the prototype of Mr. Keaton's characterization. The raiders wished to make their way to Chattanooga, burning their bridges behind them, and tearing up the tracks as they trekked over them, in an attempt to prevent the Southern army from succoring the Tennessee city.

The pages of one history book mention a young engineer who chased the whole lot of them, both as a duty to the South and to rescue his iron friend and companion, "The General." This engineer comes out of history's pages in the frozen-faced guise of Buster Keaton.

This youth belonged to the ranks of the heroes of 1862, Northerners and Southerners, who chaffed under the tasks imposed upon them by their respective superiors. Like so many others, the gallant engineer yearned for glory in the first line of fighting, only to be told that a man who could run a crack railway locomotive like "The General" should do nothing else but.

Something of the proportions upon which modern motion-picture production is done can be had from the fact that the Keaton company not only hired thousands of extra performers for Union and Confederate soldier roles and parts of citizens in the section where the raid occurred but that many miles of specially built railroads were utilized and several old locomotives rebuilt into engines of the types used during the Civil War. In addition, scores of technically perfect passenger coaches and freight cars were constructed.

BUSTER KEATON'S NEW FILM COMING TO·········

The biggest comedy in the history of the motion picture industry is coming to the..........................Theatre......................!

It is "The General," Buster Keaton's first United Artists starring vehicle.

Combining thrills which have never been equaled in the dramatic field with the most laughs of Keaton's career, "The General" is said to sound a new, dominant note in the comedy world. Produced by Joseph M. Schenck, chairman of the board of directors of the United Artists Corporation, the huge fun film is acknowledged to be the costliest comedy ever made.

Thousands appear in the supporting cast, which is headed by Marian Mack, a young actress who temporarily abandoned a starring career in dramatic pictures to become Buster's leading lady. Miss Mack contends that a leading role in a Keaton United Artists production gives her comedy experience necessary for permanent stardom.

"The General" is one picture in which historical accuracy has been preserved without sacrificing laughs.

Based on the famous Andrews railroad raid and locomotive chase during the Civil War, the comedy treats the lighter side of the struggle between the States without burlesquing any of the historical episodes. Several battles are re-enacted on the screen in unfolding the story of a young Confederate daredevil who at the start of the war is refused enlistment in the Southern army because of his value to the cause as a railroad engineer.

When a band of Northern raiders steal a train and attempt to penetrate into Confederate territory, tearing up track and destroying lines of communication, Buster, fearing for the safety of his beloved locomotive, "The General," and to rescue his sweetheart, a prisoner of the foe, pursues them.

One of the sensational scenes in the case is the plunge of a locomotive from a burning trestle into a river. This one thrill alone cost $40,000 to make.

As an illustration of the magnitude of the production of "The General" it might be mentioned that the Keaton company purchased three locomotives and dozens of coaches, converted them into Civil War period equipment, and leased several miles of track in the Pacific Northwest.

Actual camera work on "The General" required more than six months.

More than 200,000 feet of film was shot" in making "The General," Buser Keaton's big comedy spectacle at the .... Theatre. From this mass of swift and hilarious action Buster and his staff of editors and cutters selected the 7,000 odd feet in the film.

Good Ones Before Opening

MY IDEA OF THE IDEAL GIRL

By BUSTER KEATON

(Star of "The General at the .... Theatre)

Close your eyes and watch me closely, folks. I have nothing concealed up my sleeve, and if you know lip reading, it should be easy to say the titles out loud without disturbing your neighbor.

I agree perfectly with the late Mons. Munchausen that the first perquisite of the ideal tribute payer to the bobber is that she is able to play pinochle. This insures fiances and husbands against getting pneumonia and hoof and mouth complaint when they are forced to leave the fireside on rainy nights to attend business conferences downtown.

The "I'll Deal" girl also keeps the game speeded up and prevents the heavy winner from suddenly remembering that he promised to be home in time to prepare the police dog's breakfast.

My I. of the I. G. always insists on the rugs being sprinkled with cigar, cigarette and pipe ashes. In fact, she would be expected to tip over a few ash trays in order to make the boy friends feel at ease.

She also:

Reads the right-hand side of Jesse James cafe menus before ordering from the left-hand side.

Doesn't drag her spouse or sweetheart to recitals given by infant prodigies.

Calls the police the minute any of her guests begin reciting "The Shooting of Dan McGrew."

Waives all rights to the radio during jazz music programs and lets hubby tune in on the fight-by-rounds. Also agrees that the sport page is as important as the fashion page in the newspapers, and acts accordingly.

Demands that her handsome mate fire his homely stenographer and hire a pretty one.

Admits that the reason why she goes to Grand Opera is to see what the other women are wearing, not because she likes the show.

Has her nose all powdered, her coiffure all coiffed and her gown all gowned at the exact hour she said she would be ready for the ball, the theatre or the visit to the friends' house.

Refrains from asking foolish questions at the baseball game. Ditto— football game, boxing match and horse race.

Doesn't use expressions such as "Too bee-u-ti-ful for words!", "So dee-lish-ous, it melts in your mouth!", "Darlingest thing in the world!"

Refuses to agree with ultra-flappers that Mons. Marcel is a greater man than the inventor of the sewing machine; or that the discoverer of radium was a poor prune compared to the bird who thought up the double chocolate pecan sundae.

Disclaims having certain relatives who are handsomer than John Barrymore, prettier than Mary Pickford, more athletic than Doug Fairbanks and funnier than Charles Chaplin—needing only the chance in the movies to make the afore-said stars lose their jobs.

I can tell you where the ideal girl lives. It's in the town where the dodo birds come from; gasoline sells for five cents a gallon; talking in picture shows is punishable by boiling in oil; you always get the right number on the telephone; all trains arrive on time; and waiters and hat checkers refuse to be tipped.

Try and find it!

KEATON'S LAUGH FEAST COMING TO··········

A thousand and one laughs, plus a hundred and one thrills, plus one-mile-a-minute love affair, equals . . .

"The General," the next attraction at the........................Theatre.

Buster Keaton is responsible for the biggest comedy spectacle ever brought to the screen, a humorous story of the Civil War that took nearly a year to make, cost a fortune, utilized the services of thousands of people and necessitated the purchase of three locomotives and scores of cars for conversion into ante-bellum railroad equipment.

The huge laugh opus deals with the lighter chapters of the struggle between the States.

Buster, who directed his first United Artists feature, which was produced by Joseph M. Schenck, is a young Southerner who pilots one of the crack trains running through Tennessee and Georgia during the early sixties.

The outbreak of hostilities finds him anxious to leave civil life and join the Confederates at the front, but the military leaders secretly decree otherwise and decide he is of more value to the cause as an engineer. This brings complications, for his sweetheart, her family and the rest of the Southerners brand him as a slacker.

The youth gets his chance to prove he is made of heroic stuff when a band of Northerners steal "The General" and dash through Tennessee and Georgia with the wood-burning locomotive, destroying track, bridges and telegraph wires. Buster chases them, repairing the damage as he goes. How he finally foils the enemy by plunging a locomotive from a burning bridge into a river and giving warning to the Confederates in time to avert a military disaster forms a climax that is as thrilling as it is mirth-provoking.

Keaton's big supporting cast in "The General" is headed by Marian Mack, one of Hollywood's best known leading ladies, who has the role of a Confederate belle.

BUSTER KEATON NOT "THE GENERAL" AFTER ALL

In April of 1862 the famous Andrews railroad raid took place at Big Shanty, Ga., and much of the fun in Keaton's new comedy centers upon that basic incident. It was fashionable in the days when skirts were skirts and America didn't need a good five cent cigar to christen your pet locomotive with a symbolic name. So the crack railway snorter of Big Shanty was baptized "The General."

Buster plays the part of the young engineer, an actual character in history, who was so attached to his iron friend and companion, "The General," that he chased a score of Union daredevils over burning bridges and torn-up tracks, even inside the Federal lines.

"The General" is the costliest comedy spectacle ever made and is Keaton's first picture for United Artists. Directed by Buster himself, the comedy was produced by Joseph M. Schenck.

"BIOGRAPH BABY" BACK IN FILMS WITH KEATON

Ross McCutcheon, who portrays one of the northern raiders in Buster Keaton's Civil War comedy spectacle, "The General," at the ....Theatre, was the original "Biograph Baby" in the early days of motion pictures.

Young McCutcheon played in the famous company which gave present day notables such as D. W. Griffith and Mack Sennett their starts.

McCutcheon left the Biograph Company to appear on the legitimate stage with Willie Collier, Sr.

He served during the World War and spent five years on the stage after the end of hostilities before again entering motion pictures.

McCutcheon narrowly escaped death when he swam a rapids during the filming of a spectacular scene in "The General," which was produced by Joseph M. Schenck as Keaton's first picture for United Artists.

Buster Keaton had a double responsibility in making "The General," for he directed his own most ambitious starring vehicle.

General Advance Stories

BUSTER KEATON COMING IN "THE GENERAL"

"Frozen-Face" In Civil War Comedy Spectacle To Be Shown At........................ Theatre

Buster Keaton,—he of the frozen face,—comes to the .... Theatre next week in "The General," his great comedy spectacle of the sixties, the comedian's most pretentious effort. "The General" cost $500,000 to produce and it is Buster's first United Artists picture, placing him in the same category with Mary Pickford, Gloria Swanson, Charlie Chaplin, Douglas Fairbanks, John Barrymore and other dominating film stars who comprise United Artists membership.

"The General" is based on actual historical fact. The Andrews Railroad Raid of 1862 inspired the comedian to make a huge comedy spectacle, with thousands of soldiers and lavish sets in nature's studio, with three Civil War railroad engines bumping over the ties and jouncing audiences out of their seats with laughter. Marian Mack, a brunette, is the Southern belle for whom the gallant Buster stakes his shirt,—the grey flannel one.

Nearly all of the action is hilarious, swift-moving railroad fun, with Buster as the engineer of The General, an historic engine of the sixties, which chased and was chased by another iron horse all over the countryside. In one scene an engine nose dives into a river,—and $40,000 of Joseph M. Schenck's money went with it for a one-minute thrill on the screen. Mr. Schenck and Buster were unanimous in their decision to film the scene as realistically as possible. Buster leaped from the cab just in time to save the film business one of its greatest assets.

Unlike many comedies, "The General" has a real love story running through it, a breath-taking, hair-raising tale of soldiers and engines and sweethearts and a face that never smiles. The girl thinks Buster is a slacker because the recruiting officer thinks an engineer more valuable to the South than a foot soldier. But Buster shows her, and how!

Manager .... of the ....Theatre announced yesterday that he felt the .... Theatre honored in offering to its . patrons Buster Keaton's first independent production, a comedy so chock-full of entertainment values, thrills, suspense and hilarious situations that only a Keaton could keep a straight face in watching it.

"Buster wanted to make his first independent film a big picture, something surpassing anything he had done before," said Manager ...., "and I'm sure everyone will agree he did it."

"The General" was nearly a year in production. It cost a few thousand dollars more than an even half million dollars. Most of the vast scenes depicted were taken near Cottage Grove, Ore., which Buster decided after three months' travelling in the South and West, was the spot most resembling the Big Shanty, Ga., of 1862. In the South where the original incident of the Andrews Railroad Raid occurred, native industry and subsequent prosperity during the past half century have builded the region so rapidly that, as Buster says, "You'd never know the old place now." So he went up to Oregon, built replicas of Big Shanty, Kingston and other towns which figure in the action of the film, and after six months' production work in the great outdoors, brought forth "The General" for audiences at the .... Theatre to view.

General Advance Stories

BUSTER KEATON HELPED N. G. O. RECRUITING

Recruiting for the Oregon National Guard recently was given an impetus when Buster Keaton made "The General," his first big comedy for United Artists, many of the scenes of which were filmed in the Pacific Northwest. "The General" is the feature film at the..........................Theatre this week.

Oregon state officials co-operated with the Keaton company by permitting the frozen-faced star to use several companies of militia for the Civil War battle scenes. Word went out that National Guardsmen would be given a chance to display their prowess in motion pictures, and within two days after the announcement was made, the recruiting offices were besieged by swarms of men and youths.

The National Guard companies were recruited to full strength, hundreds of aspirants being rejected. Officials estimated that Keaton would have had the use of 10,000 soldiers if he had needed that many.

Several companies of the Reserve Officers' Training Corps also were used in re-enacting the Civil War battles which play an important part of the gigantic laugh feature.

The soldiers took the parts of the thousands of Confederate and Union cavalry and infantry in "The General," which, although a comedy, does not in any way burlesque the struggle between the States. The picture is based on the lighter chapters of the Civil War, much of the plot centering around the historic Andrews railroad raid and locomotive chase. Three wood-burning locomotives of the type which snorted over the rails during the sixties play a prominent part in "The General."

One scene alone—the plunge of an engine through a burning trestle—cost $40,000 to make.

BUSTER KEATON BUILT A TOWN FOR MOVIE

Buster Keaton: Town Builder.

The famous frozen-faced comedian had to essay that role when he made "The General," his first United Artists Picture, which is playing at the................ Theatre.

The story is built around the lighter chapters of the Civil War. Most of the action takes place in Tennessee and Georgia during the sixties, and because of the progress of the South since the struggle between the States, it was necessary to seek elsewhere for virgin territory in which to construct entire towns, a railroad, bridges and other properties incident to the historical comedy.

After traveling more than 9,000 miles in search of location, Buster and his technical staff selected a strip of wooded, mountainous country in Oregon for "The General." Keaton personally supervised the construction of the sets, which required several weeks to erect. Replicas of Tennessee and Georgia towns as they appeared during the sixties were built along the right-of-way of the railroad leased by Keaton. Several trainloads of materials were used.

At the height of activity in the Keaton camp, the population of the towns totaled thousands, but when "The General" was completed and the Keaton company had departed for Hollywood, the towns resembled ghost cities. Some of the material used in the construction of the towns was salvaged. The skeletons of the motion picture cities still remain in Oregon as mute reminders of their brief days of glory in bringing the lighter side of the Civil War to the screen.

Produced by Joseph M. Schenck for United Artists, "The General" was directed by the frozen-faced star and Clyde Bruckman. The large supporting cast is headed by Marian Mack, who has the role of a Confederate belle. Many other well known screen players appear in the comedy spectacle.

General Advance Stories

KEATON'S LOCOMOTIVES NOT FROM A TOY SHOP

Buster Keaton recently went shopping for locomotives!

Not toy ones, but real iron horses weighing many tons each.

Keaton needed the locomotives for his first United Artists picture, "The General," a comedy spectacle with a Civil War background, which comes to the........................Theatre.................. When he found three of the type he wanted, he rebuilt them into replicas of engines that snorted over the rails during the 60's. He also acquired many old freight cars and passenger coaches for conversion into Civil War period rolling stock.

- In filming the costliest and most ambitious comedy in the history of the motion picture industry, Keaton assembled equipment and historical data from all parts of the country. Although primarily planned for laughing purposes only, "The General" is technically accurate from an historical standpoint, and was filmed on a scale attempted in in but few dramatic productions.

Buster Keaton, star of "The General," finds recreation in his radio; while his leading lady, Marian Mack, finds hers in her bicycle.

$500,000 KEATON COMEDY COMING TO·········

Acclaimed as the costliest and most lavish comedy ever produced, "The General," Buster Keaton's laugh and thrill feature of the Civil War comes to the ....Theatre........................

"The General" is unique in filmdom, in that it picturizes a true story of the sixties, is historically accurate, contains thrills never duplicated in the biggest dramatic photoplays, and at the same time is comedy from the opening fade-in to the final fade-out.

When Buster started work on "The General" as his first picture for United Artists, he did so with the idea of making the year's biggest comedy. When critical Hollywood audiences previewed the completed opus they pronounced it not only the greatest comedy they had ever seen, but a feature that ranks in dramatic action with some of the outstanding photoplays of the past decade.

Nearly a year elapsed from the time Buster and his staff began research work on "The General" until the comedy was completed. Several months were spent on location in Oregon, where Civil War towns were built, a railroad leased, three locomotives and scores of cars purchased and converted into wood-burners and equipment of the sixties, and thousands of National Guardsmen and former soldiers recruited for the battle scenes.

One of the big thrills in "The General," which is based on the Andrews railroad raid and locomotive chase, a vivid chapter of the Civil War, is the plunge of a speeding locomotive from a burning trestle into a raging river. This scene was made at a cost of $40,-000; the wreckage still reposes in the bed of the river near Cottage Grove, Oregon.

Personally directed by the star and photographed by several of the best-known cameramen, "The General" was produced by Joseph M. Schenck.

HERALDS THAT BRING 'EM IN

A good herald is your most important accessory. — Here is a dand
— forceful and attractive — a showman's idea of pulling powe

Order From Your Nearest Supply Depot

ATLANTA, GA.	Dowman & Wilkins	107 Luckie St.,
BOSTON, MASS.	Grenier Print Shop	210 Stuart St.,
CHARLOTTE, N. C.	Queen City Printing Co.	14 E 4th St.
CHICAGO, ILL.	Filmac Co., Inc.	730 S. Wabash Ave.

(Also Supplies Indianapolis and Minneapolis Territories)

CLEVELAND, OHIO	Wolkoff Printing Co.	1104 Prospect Ave.
CINCINNATI, OHIO	Enquirer Job Printing Co.	412 East 6th St.,
DALLAS, TEXAS	Steinmacher & Clark	2715 Elm St.,
DETROIT, MICH.	Cinema Service Co.	141 E. Elizabeth St.
INDIANAPOLIS, IND.	(See Chicago)	
KANSAS CITY, MO.	Keystone Press	19th & Wyandotte
LOS ANGELES, CALIF.	Acorn Press	2020 S. Vermont Ave.,
MINNEAPOLIS, MINN.	(See Chicago)	
NEW HAVEN, CONN.	Hoffman Press	163 State St.,
NEW YORK, N. Y.	The Longacre Press, Inc.	427 W. 42nd St.
OMAHA, NEB.	Waters-Barnhart Printing Co.	414 S. 13th St.
PHILADELPHIA, PA.	Triangle Printing Co.	1015 Winter St.,
PITTSBURGH, PA.	Exhibitors Program Co.	1006 Forbes St.,
SALT LAKE CITY, UTAH	Quality Press	American Bldg.,
SAN FRANCISCO, CALIF.	Western Poster Co.	117 Goldengate Ave.
SEATTLE, WASH.	Western Poster Co.	1929 Third Ave.
WASHINGTON, D. C.	The Printcraft Shop	108 Second St., S.W.

THE LONGACRE PRESS, INC.

Publishers of all United Artists Heralds

427-431 WEST 42ND STREET   NEW YORK

Prices on all United Artists Heralds

1,000 to 5,000 at $3.75 per M
6,000 to 10,000 at 3.50 per M
11,000 or over at 3.25 per M

AUTOGRAPH PORTRAIT

(Size 5 x 7)

Order Direct from

WALCO PICTORIAL COMPANY

522 Park Avenue, West New York, N. J.

100	$ 1.50 per hundred
1,000 to 5,000	13.50 per thousand
6,000 to 10,000	11.50 per thousand
10,000	10.00 per thousand

NOTE—A brief biography of Buster Keaton is printed on the back of each portrait, with blank space below amply large for a theatre imprint. These 5 x 7 Buster Keaton portraits make ideal souvenirs for distribution.

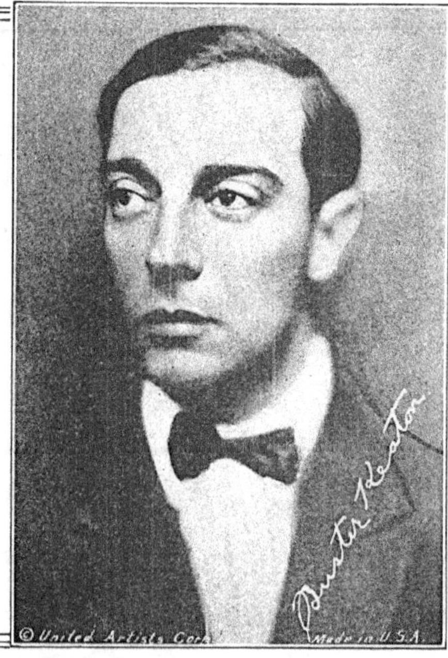

Order Your Accessories Here for

BUSTER KEATON

IN

"THE GENERAL"

United Artists Picture

Send to

Manager ____________________________________

Name of Theatre ____________________________________

Town ____________________________ State ____________________

THE GENERAL—Order Blank	Price	How Many	Amount
POSTERS (Lithographed):			
One Sheet, No. 1	$0.12		
One Sheet, No. 2	.12		
Three Sheet, No. 1	.36		
Three Sheet, No. 2	.36		
Six Sheet	.72		
Twenty-four Sheet	2.00		
WINDOW CARDS (Lithographed)	.10		
LOBBY DISPLAY CARDS:			
Hand Colored 22 x 28, each	.40		
Hand Colored 11 x 14 (Set of eight)	.75		
INSERT CARD (Hand Colored) 14 x 36, each	.25		
In lots of 50 or over, each	.20		
BLACK and WHITE SQUEEGEE PHOTOS, 8 x 10			
Lobby Set (25 in set)	2 50		
Newspaper Set (25 in set)	2.50		
Single copies squeegee photos	.10		
SLIDE No. 1	.15		
SLIDE No. 2	.15		

	Mats	Cuts	
BK-0—Thumbnail Sketch	x	$0.20	
BK-1—One-Column Portrait	$0.05	.30	
BK-2—Two-Column Portrait	.10	.50	
BK-3—One-Column Sketches (four)	.10	x	
BK-4—One-Column Sketch	.05	x	
BK-5—One-Column Scene	.05	.30	
BK-6—One-Column Scene	.05	.30	
BK-7—Two-Column Scene	.10	.50	
BK-8—Two-Column Scene	.10	.50	
BK-9—Two-Column Sketch	.10	x	
BK-10—Two-Column Engine	.10	x	
BKX—Two-Column Time Table	.10	.50	
BK-11—Four-Column Cannon	.30	x	
BK-12—Six-Column Cartoons (Set of six)	1 00	x	
BKD-13—One-Column Ad Slug	.05	x	
BKD-14—One-Column Ad	.05	30	
BKD-15—One-Column Ad	.05	.30	
BKD-16—Two-Column Ad Slug	.10	x	
BKD-17—Two-Column Ad	.10	.50	
BKD-18—Two-Column Ad	.10	.50	
BKD-19—Three-Column Ad	.20	x	
BKD-20—Four-Column Ad	.30	x	

Total . . . .

These Prices Prevail for United States only

"LAUGH PANIC" OF THRILLS

BALLY-HOOS

A LOCOMOTIVE of the type used in "The General" can be constructed over an automobile chassis for use on the street. Dress the driver like Buster. A sure fire stunt.

A BICYCLE, high wheeled, such as Buster rides in the picture, is a logical attention attractor. Easy enough to make of buggy wheels and to ride.

SANDWICHMEN garbed in the quaint costumes of the Sixties (stovepipe hats, frock coats and strap pantaloons) make an effective ballyhoo.

A MORTAR and cannon balls on a float with a figure of Buster clowning about it makes a sensational street attraction. See Still No. 62 or No. 74.

"YANKS" AND "REBS," represented by two men in costume might escort a Buster Keaton character about the streets as a prisoner.

A "HALF - AND - HALF" General on horseback will draw attention. One half his uniform is gray and the other half is blue, divided in the middle.

SPECIAL NIGHTS

For Special Nights, cooperation in railroad circles is appropriate. Likely angles are indicated in the Brotherhood of Locomotive Engineers, the Trainmen, etc. Where there are General Offices of a railroad in the city, you can make a similar point of interest for the large clerical staffs.

Wherever advisable, special G. A. R. or Confederate Veteran performances may be promoted.

An American Legion Night or a Boy Scouts Matinee or a Boy Scouts Field Day each has its value.

INTEREST WOMEN!

Start a newspaper discussion in which the grandmothers defend the crinoline and hoopskirts of the Civil War period. They will assert that the misses of '62 were just as active as the flappers of today. The modern girls may contend that the dresses of old may have been picturesque but uninspiring.

Another discussion can center around the long hair of '62 versus modern bob; the bustle versus the boyish form; the plump figure versus the slim; long skirts versus the short.

CONTESTS

ANDREWS RAID essays could be written by school children. Offer prizes for the best description of this historic incident upon which "The General" is built, the data to be obtained from authentic literature. Get public library cooperation with a list of reference books.

"JOKES OF '62" provide material for a contest. Offer rewards for the best "Yank and Reb" jokes remembered or dug up from the newspaper files of the period. A variation of this is to have Vets contribute their funniest reminiscences of the olden army camps.

TRAIN CALLING contests, on the order of the popular "hog calling" contests staged in the Middle West theatres, are appropriate as added attractions to "The General." Get your stentorian railroad brakemen and depot callers to compete, the audiences to decide the most melodious or loudest callers.

"REBEL YELLS" can be made a competition similar to the above in Southern sections where candidates are likely to be accomplished in the art.

BIG RETURNS FROM A MODEL - MAKING CONTEST

For sure-enough, worthwhile exploitation results, nothing can beat a contest that arouses the mechanical ingenuity of our younger public. The contest should culminate with finished models ready to make a big display when your play date comes, and when big cumulative interest has been developd for your show.

Tie up with a newspapr with an award for the best wooden models of an old-time railroad engine like "The General." Let manual training classes and home workshops compete. Offer added prizes for tenders, box cars, etc., for the less skillful. Give everyone time to compete.

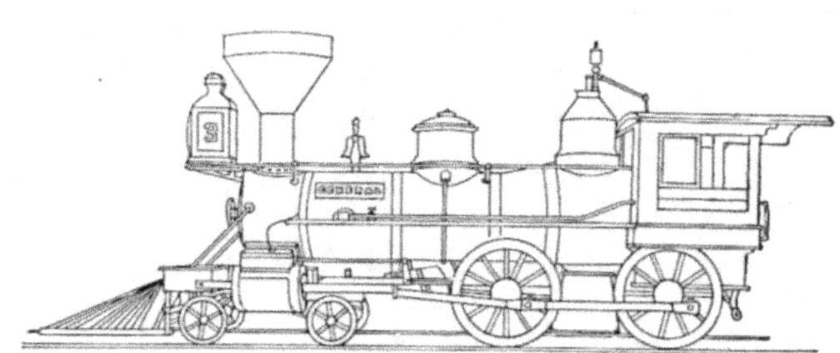

BK-10—Two-Column Engine MAT ONLY (Mat 10 cents)

(This sketch is designed as a guide for contestants in preparing models. Use it in newspaper copy in connection with a contest, or distribute it on hand bills and throwaways. The cut can also be printed in your program in order to give the contest added circulation.)

STAGE AN "1862" EXHIBIT

Go after a piece of novelty for a show window or a lobby display. Assemble a collection of relics of the period, these illustrated on this page being only a few of the possibilities. Headline the display: RELICS OF 1862—Used in BUSTER KEATON'S Spectacular Comedy "The General." Interest is added by marking each object with a humorous caption. (Note—No mats or cuts of these illustrations are available.)

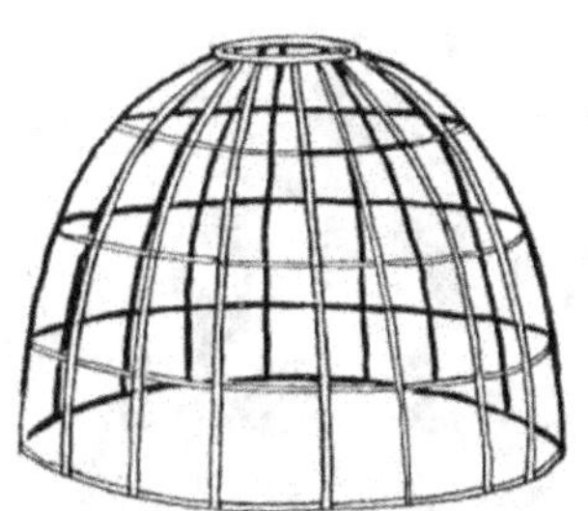

THE HOOPSKIRT

Ladies perambulated in skirts which were draped over a frame like this, and wore pantalettes to mask the ankles. On windy days all you saw was all you saw.

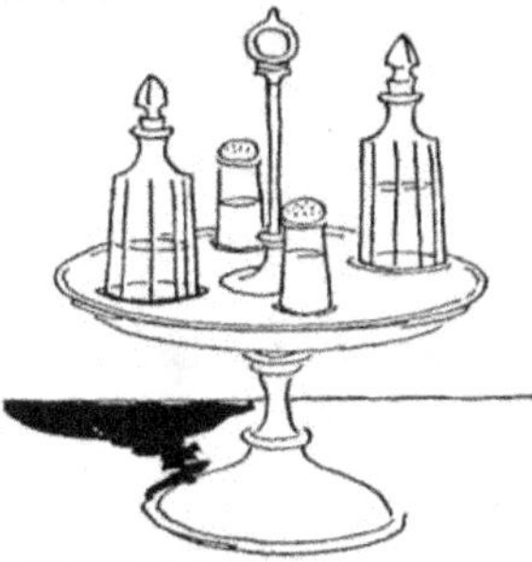

CRUET STAND

No dining room was complete without one of these obstructions to reaching across the boarding house table. They became unpopular because too many boarders were wounded while reaching.

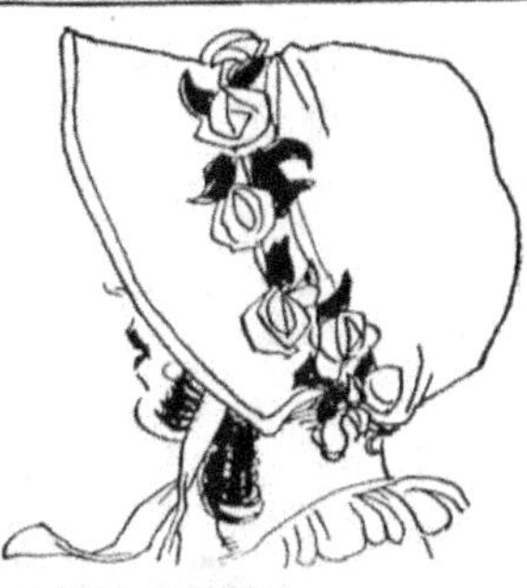

POKE BONNET

This headgear comes in every ten years, but it really flourished in 1862. The answer is that you can't spoil a really pretty girl no matter what you put on her head or neck.

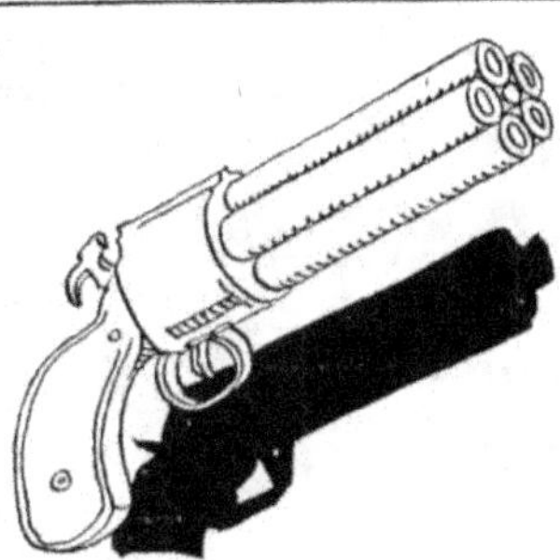

PEPPERBOX PISTOL

The barrels revolved instead of the cylinder. You saw five deaths every time you looked into the muzzle. No wonder Vicksburg fell.

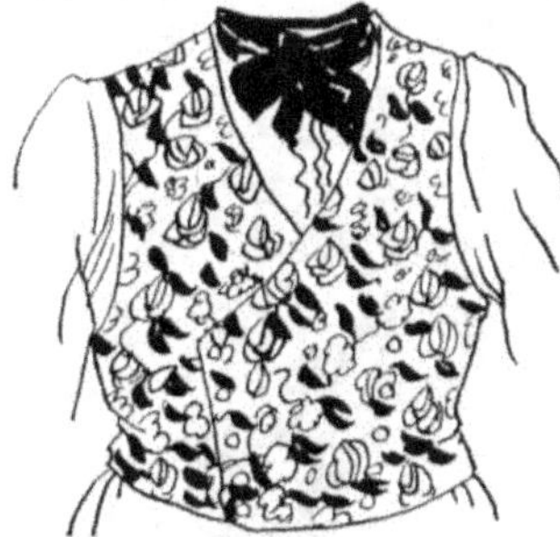

FLOWERED VEST

Everybody tried to look like a Mississippi steamboat gambler by wearing vests like this. Now they use these vests for Persian carpets.

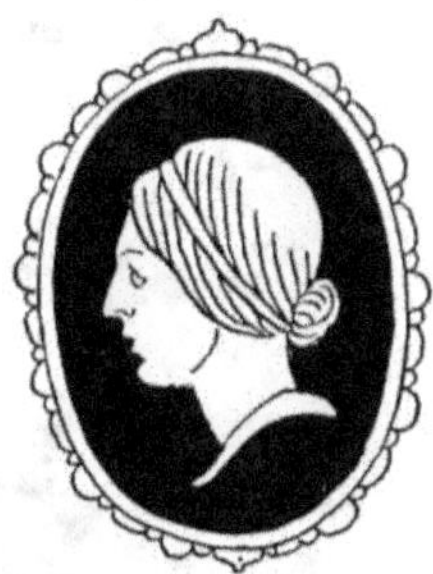

CAMEO BROOCH

That was when there was no other kind. People also wore hair watch chains, chignons and strap pantaloons. You have eighty-five guesses as to what a chignon is.

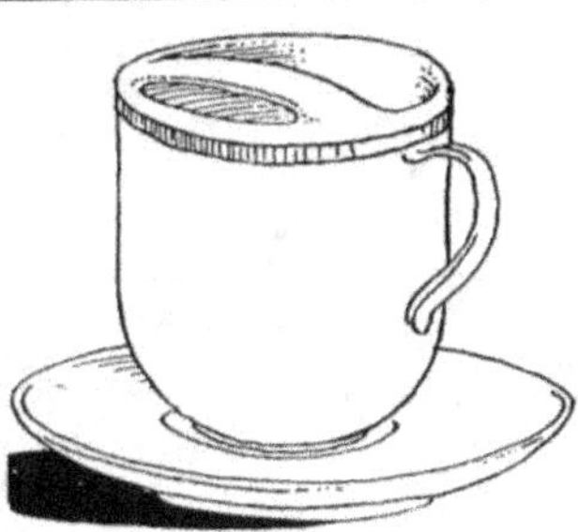

MOUSTACHE CUP

Every he-man wore hirsute soup-strainers, but was strangely finicky about coffee. When inhaling Java he insisted upon a guard rail to shield his alfalfa.

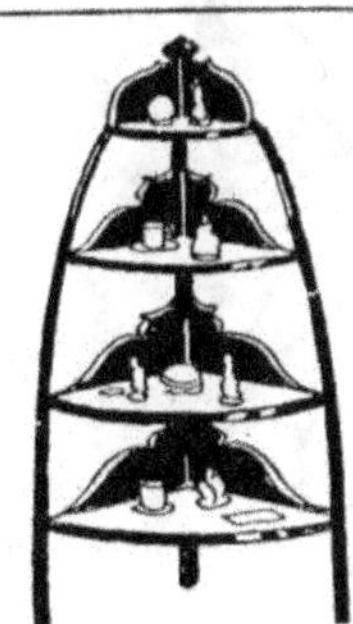

WHAT-NOT

The funniest thing about a what-not, next to its name, was that it had shelves for heirlooms. This has disappeared along with chin whiskers and cottage organs.

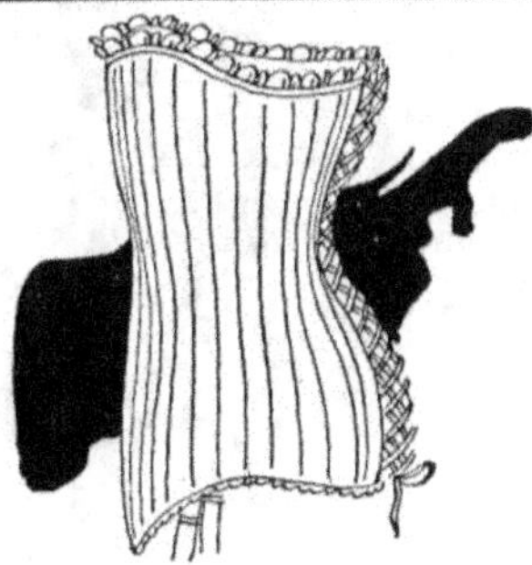

STAYS

If a woman went on the street without a whalebone corset on she felt completely undressed. Ladies never died from not wearing stays, but whaling captains had to live.

MORE RED HOT HUNCHES

PRELUDES

For a musical prelude to "The General," a modified jazzy version of "March of the Wooden Soldiers" will make a hit if the participants are dressed in blue or gray uniforms.

Railroad songs are most appropriate to a presentation and there is quite a repertory of such songs. "Casey Jones," "Alabamy Bound," "My Dad's the Engineer," "I've Been Working on the Railroad," are a few suggestions.

Old time Southern melodies can be woven into a pleasing introductory program.

Army songs also have a definite place in a prelude.

Sentimental songs of yore will apply readily to a prelude in which crinoline girls and young recruit swains could sing and dance.

USHERS

Ushers dressed as Marion Mack, heroine in "The General," will be an attractive adjunct to a presentation. The bonnet, basque and crinoline make a fetching attire.

Girls dressed as switchmen will also make a novel appearance; or they can be dressed in the Keaton engineer costume. (See Still No 17.)

CANDY STUNT

Arrange with a manufacturer to distribute sample candy kisses at the theatre Label the candy:

A Kiss from Keaton.
See Buster Keaton in "The General" and get a laugh with your kiss.

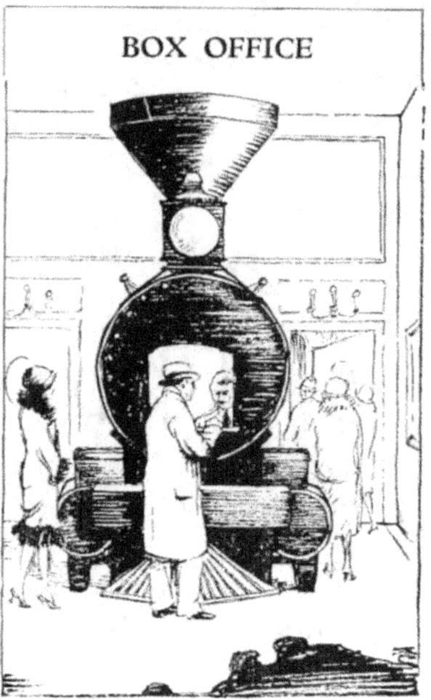

"BOX OFFICE" TIP

Frame your ticket window with a compo-board semblance of a locomotive front, following the pattern of "The General." The tickets are sold through an opening in the boiler front.

MARQUEES

In making replicas of locomotives for display, an added effect is produced by having the wheels move. Do this by rigging up a motor mechanism that will work the wheels by means of a belt.

Using a compressed air whistle and a practical engine bell on a marquee model gives your display an appeal to the ear as well as to the eye.

Suggestions for the marquee are reproductions of the Civil War locomotives used in "The General"; cardboard cutouts of Buster Keaton from the attractive line of poster material; army tents with patrolling sentinels; or a campfire scene with dummy figures representing soldiers. Many different effective lightings can be given a camp scene for night display. The same can be said for a locomotive scene where the headlight and firebox both invite electrical effects. Use a practical engine bell as a noisemaker.

A CHARACTER SKETCH OF BUSTER KEATON
by Lee Joseph Roche

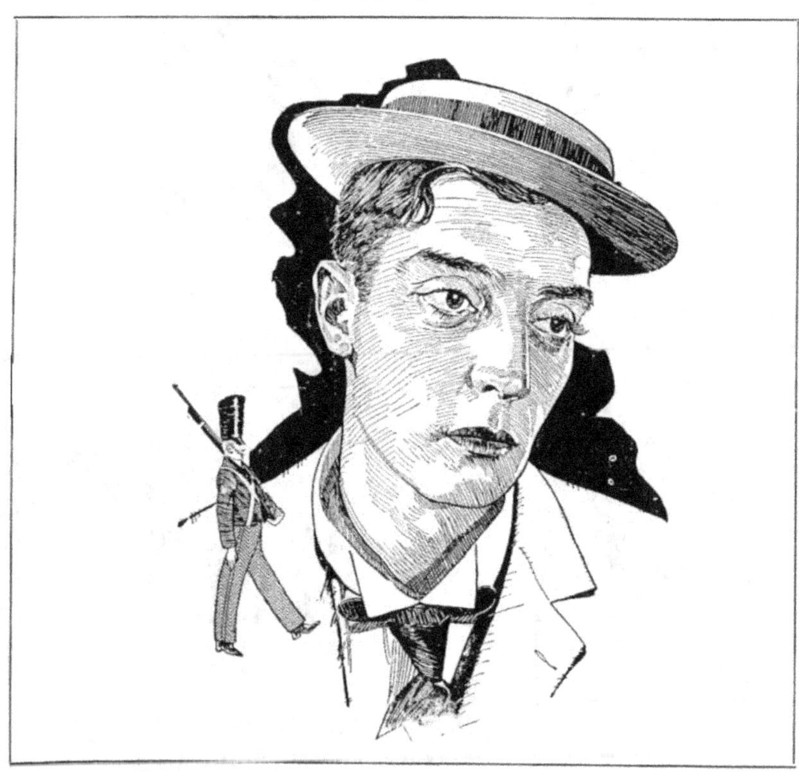

(BK-9—Two-Column Character—MATS ONLY (Mat 10c)

POWERFUL ADVERTISEMENTS FOR YOU IN CUT OR MAT FORM

BKD-17—Two Col. Adv. (Mat 10c, Cut 50c)

BKD-14—One Col. Adv. (Mat 5c, Cut 30c)

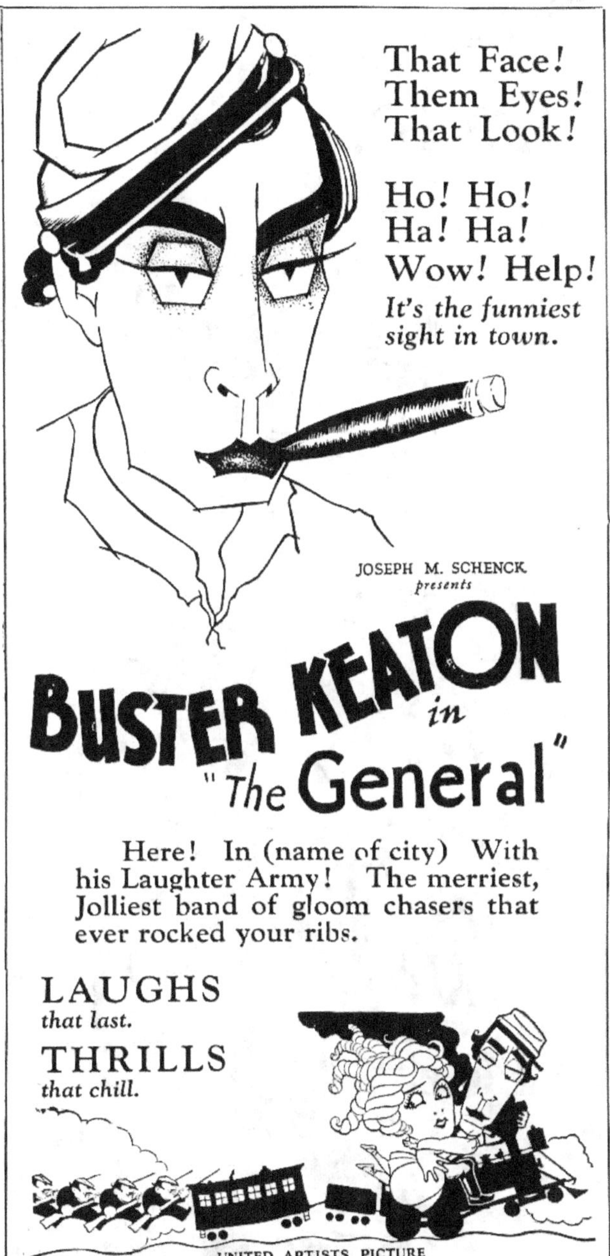

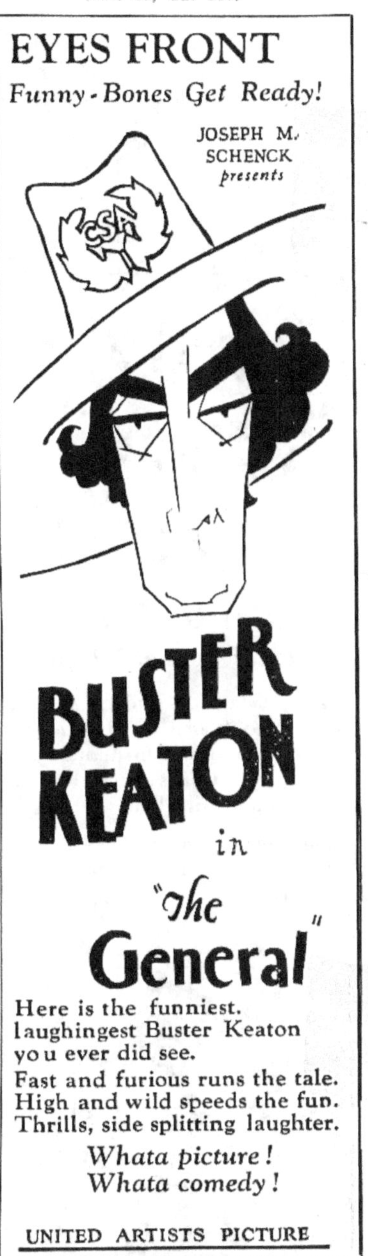

TYPE COPY <u>NOT</u> INCLUDED IN CUT OR MAT
ADDITIONAL CATCHLINES ON PAGE 15

BKD-16—Two Col. Adv. Slug (Mat 10c, No Cuts)

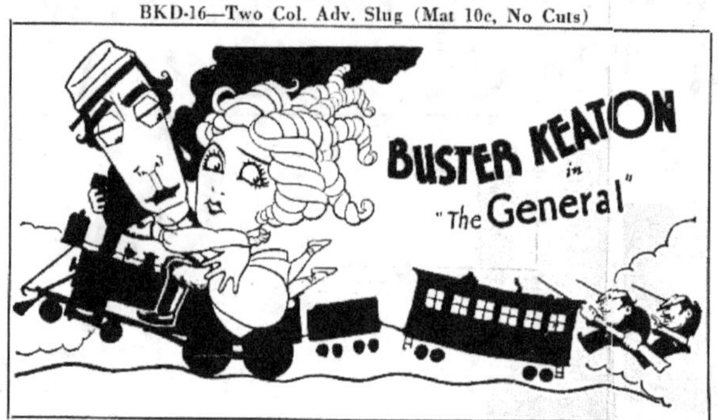

BKD-15—One Col. Adv.
(Mat 5c, Cut 30c)

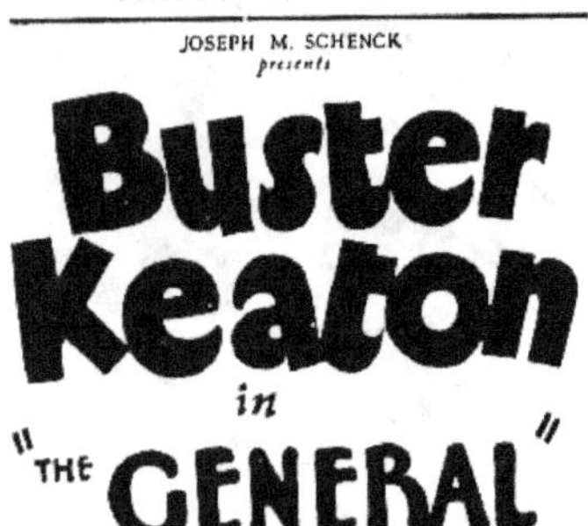

CHOO! CHOO! *The Laughter Special's Here!*

"The General" brings Buster Keaton to (name of city) in the biggest laugh and thrill show he ever made. Come ride with him! Come smile with him!

Come shake and quake with the world's famous "Frozen-Face" fun-maker.

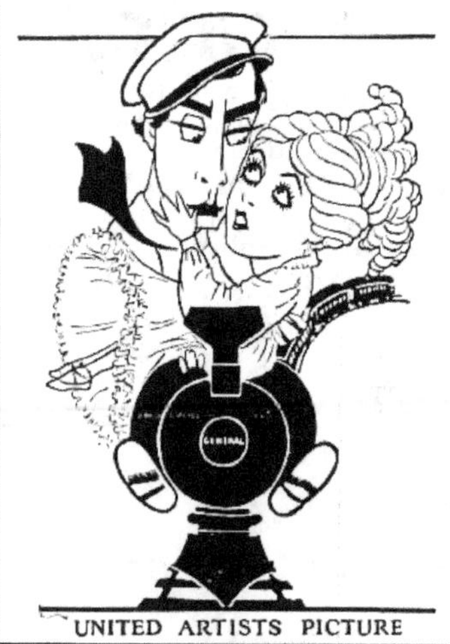

BKD-13—One Col. Adv. Slug
(Mat 5c, No Cuts)

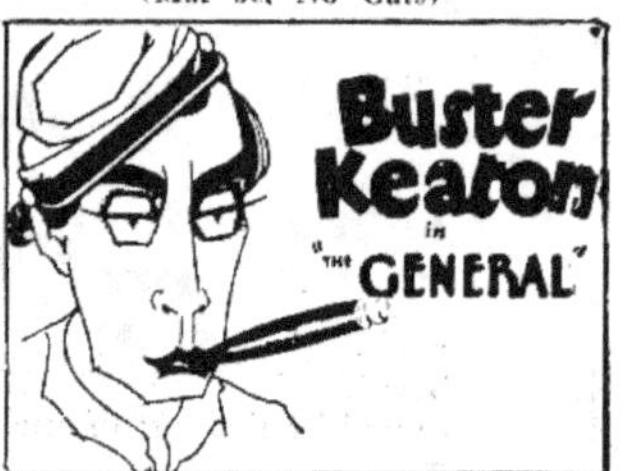

BKD-18—Two Col. Adv. (Mat 10c, Cut 50c)

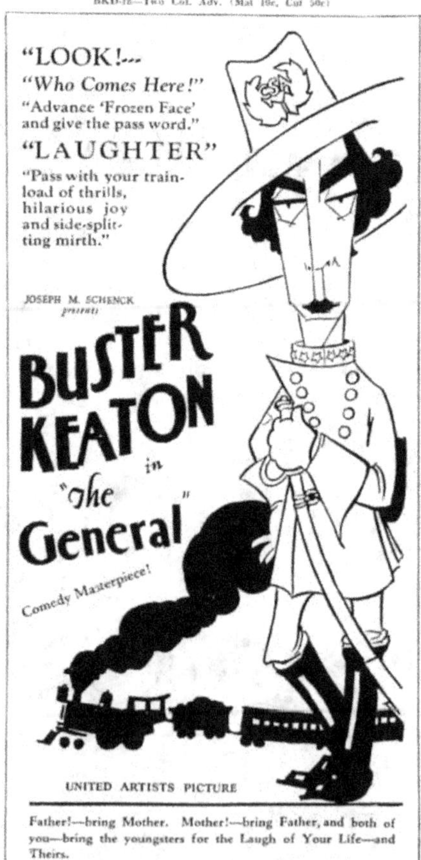

Father!—bring Mother. Mother!—bring Father, and both of you—bring the youngsters for the Laugh of Your Life—and Theirs.

BKD-19—Three Col. Adv. (Mat 20c, No Cuts)

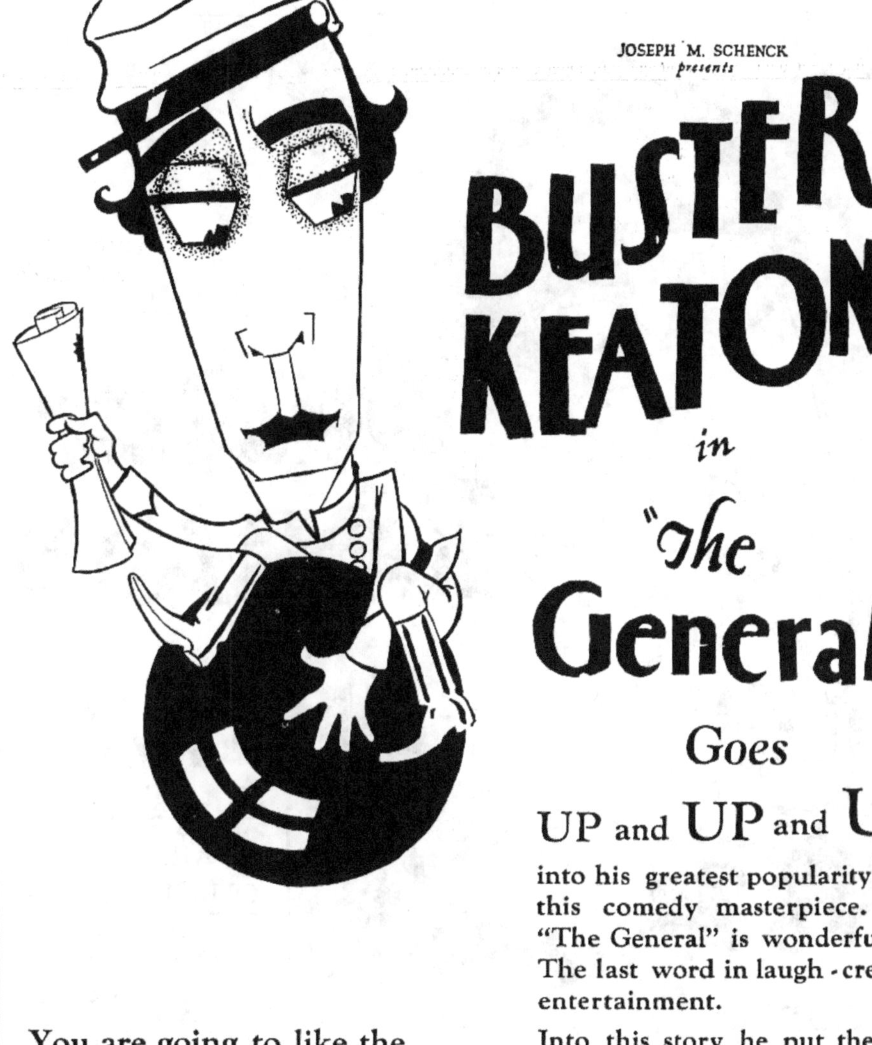

You are going to like the story because it is refreshing, clean and full of interest.

You are going to gasp and shake, shiver and quiver at his thrilling rides and daring adventures.

You'll darn near fall off your seat as Buster rolls up one tremendous laugh moment after another.

"The General" is a Laughter Leader—whose laughs last.

UNITED ARTISTS PICTURE

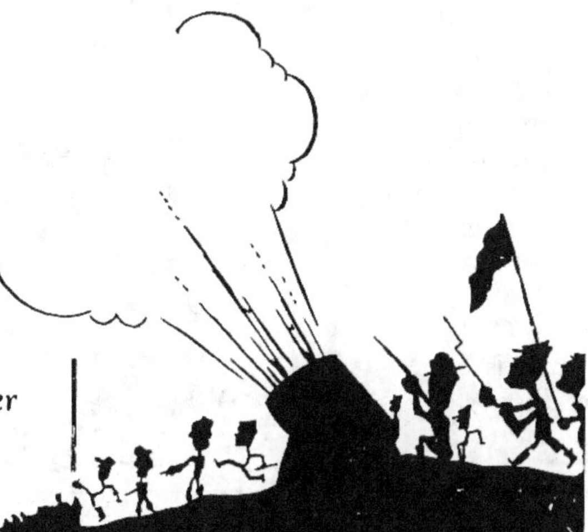

BKD-20—Four Col. Adv. (Mat 30c, No Cuts)

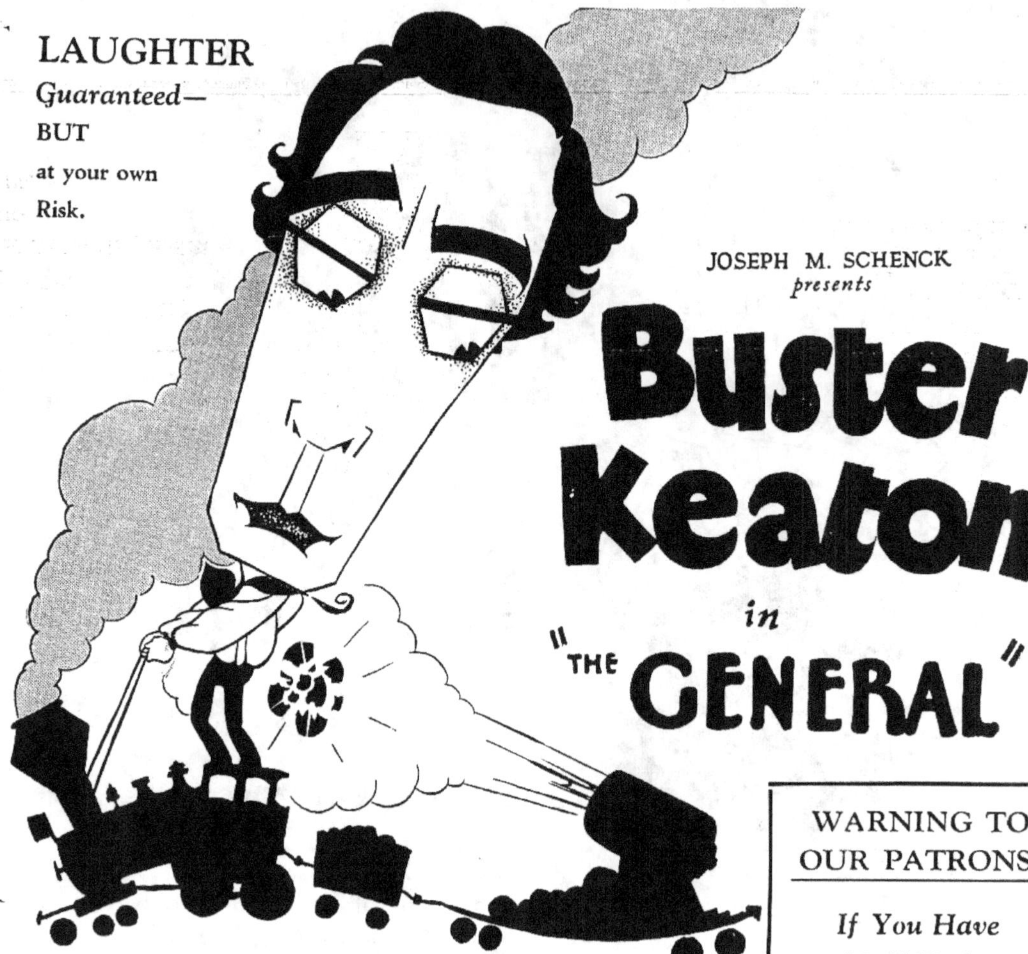

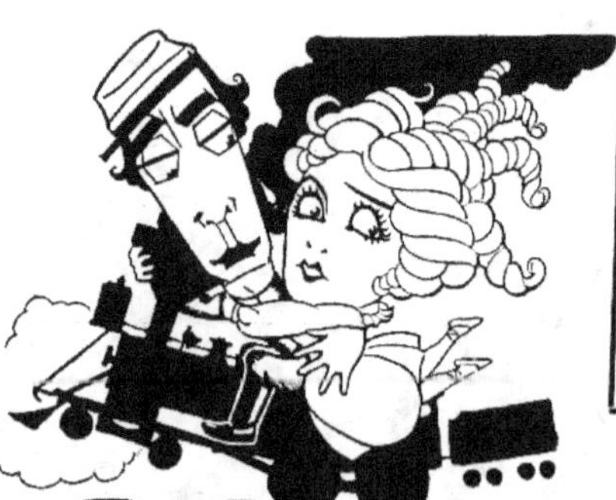

TOOT-TOOT
WHAM-BANG

Clear the track
Here comes the
Laughter Leader
The General of Joy
commanding
Private Laughs
Corporeal Laughs
Major Laughs
a Million General
    Laughs
But the Girl
commands him.
How Funny.

When the General
pulls in
GLOOM
pulls out !

WARNING TO
OUR PATRONS!

If You Have
RIBS

hyper or [super - sensitive,
kindly do not see this picture unless you have had
your ribs reinforced.

The Management will not
be responsible for ribs
bent, broken, [wrecked or
split, caused by over
laughing, over-shaking or
uncontrolled hilarity, af-
fecting any person or
persons while seeing this
production.

If you have weak ribs, see
the picture on week days.

  (Signed)
THE MANAGEMENT

UNITED ARTISTS PICTURE

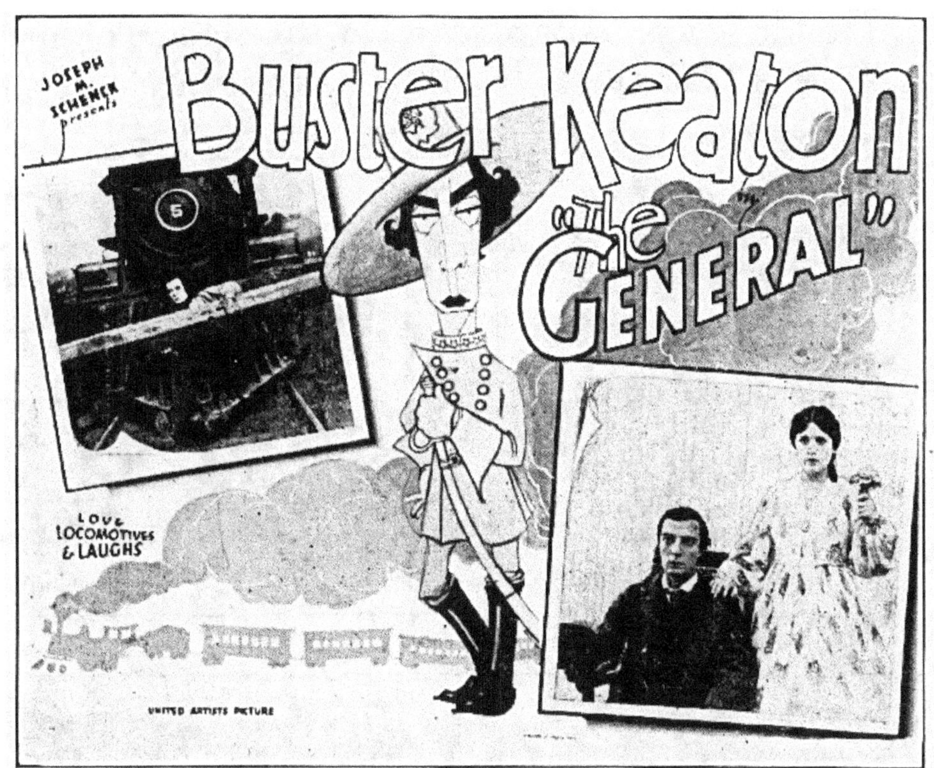

TWO 22 x 28
COLORED
LOBBY DISPLAY
Price 40 cents each
80 cents set of two

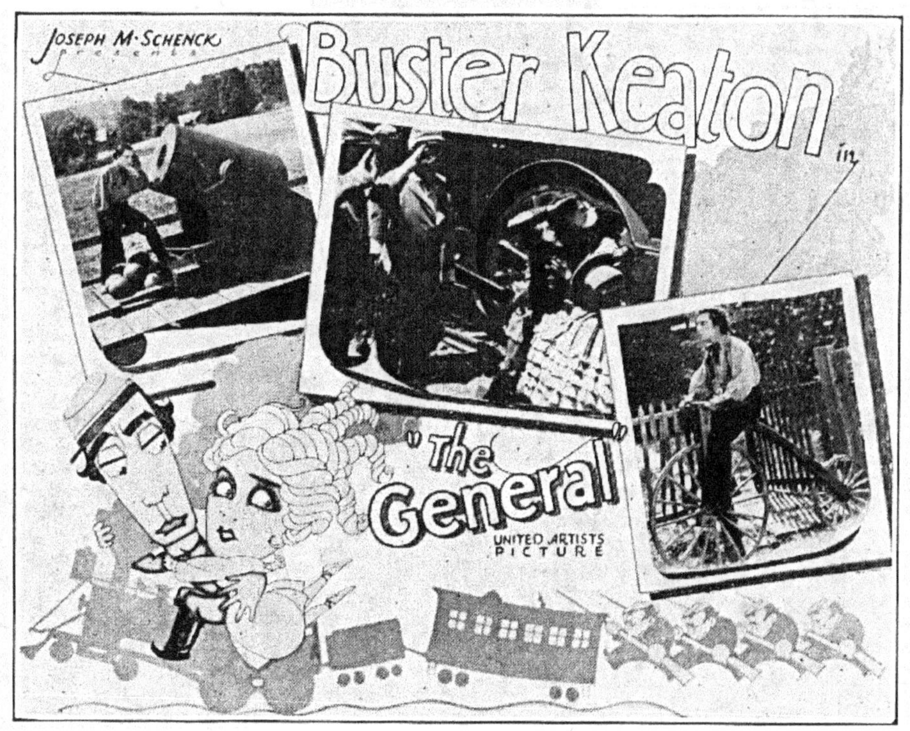

POWERFUL ADVERTISEMENTS FOR TYPE COPY NOT INCLUDED IN CUT OR MAT

For Display Advertisements
Pull Down This Page

THESE COLORED LOBBY CARDS BRING BUSINESS

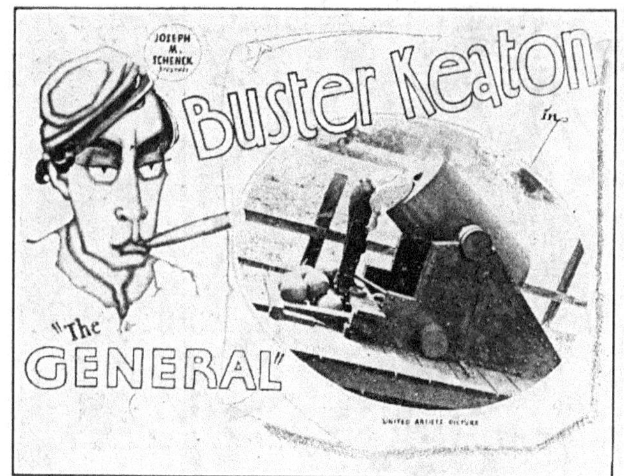

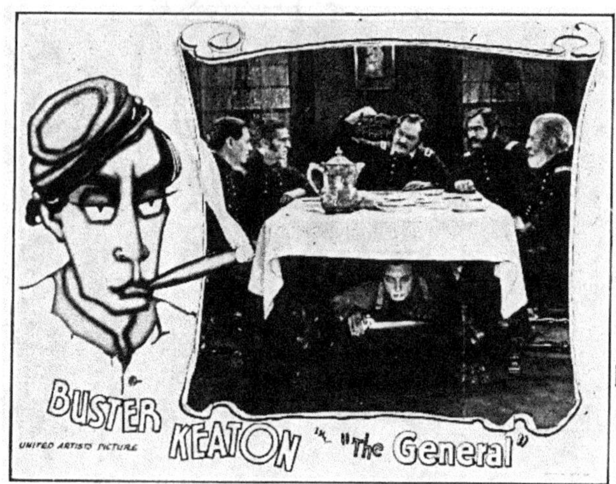

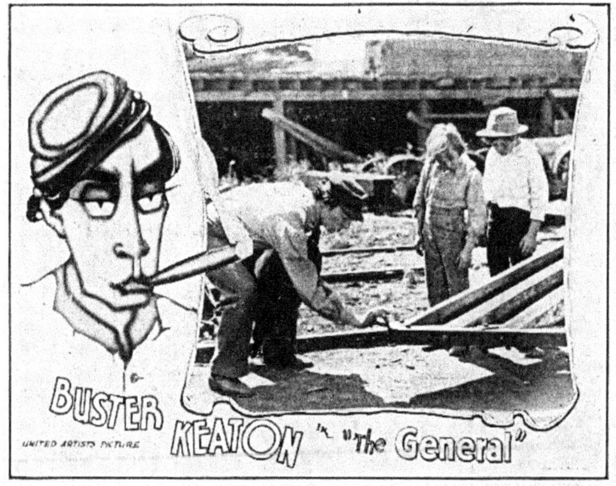

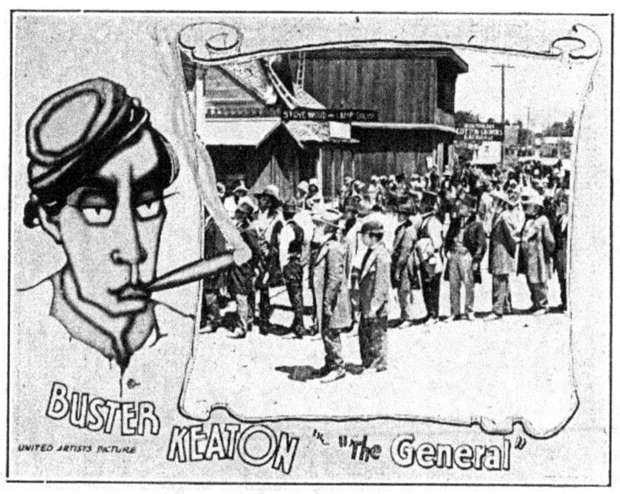

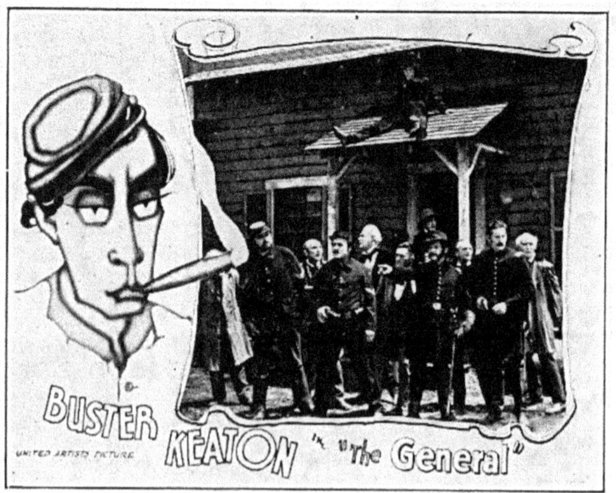

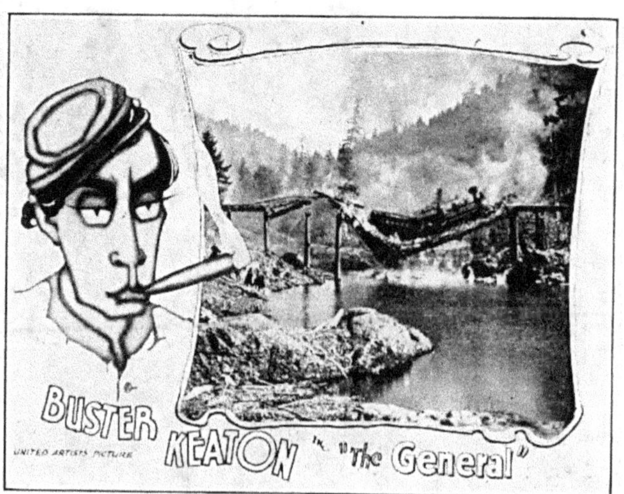

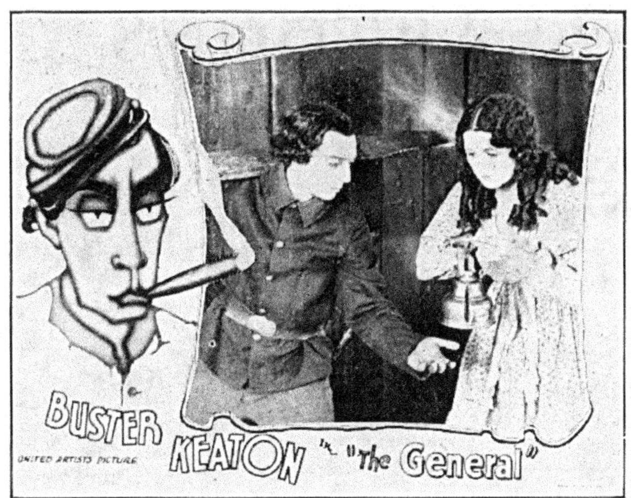

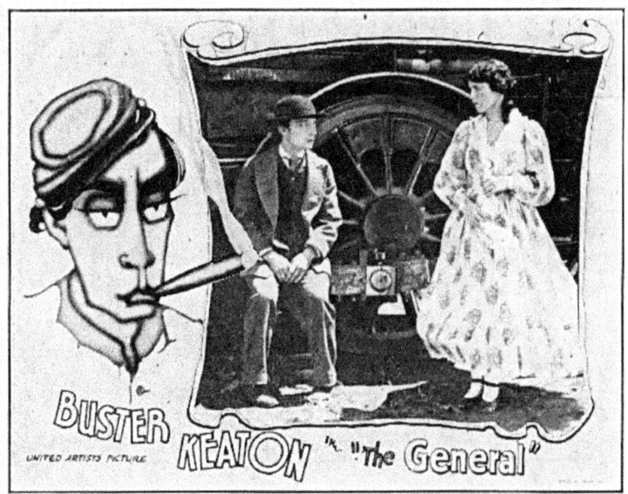

Above
EIGHT 11 x 14
COLORED
LOBBY DISPLAY
Price per Set
75 cents

TIE-UPS AND CARTOONS

John Decker, New York World cartoonist, has made a series of six special cartoons on Buster Keaton. These are shown herewith in miniature, but they are obtainable at United Artists Corporation exchanges in TWELVE-INCH width. Offer them to your newspaper to run as a comic feature. Ask for BK-12—Six Column Cartoons (Price $1.00 per set of six mats).

"LITTLE FROZEN FACE"—Empty Shoes—BUSTER KEATON in "The General."

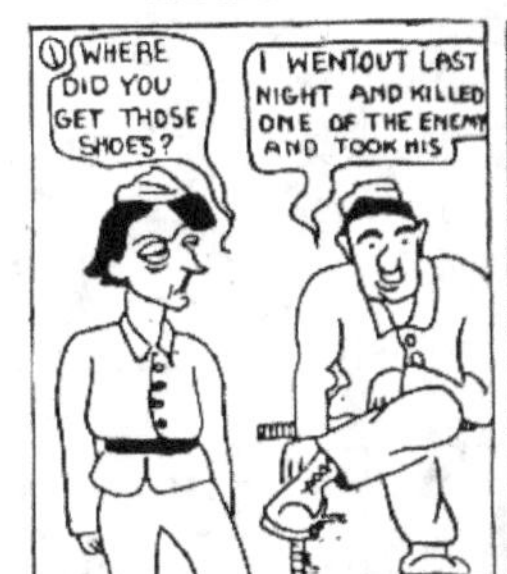

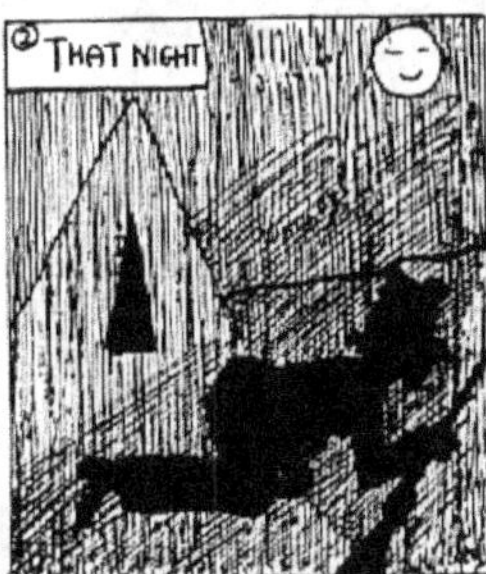

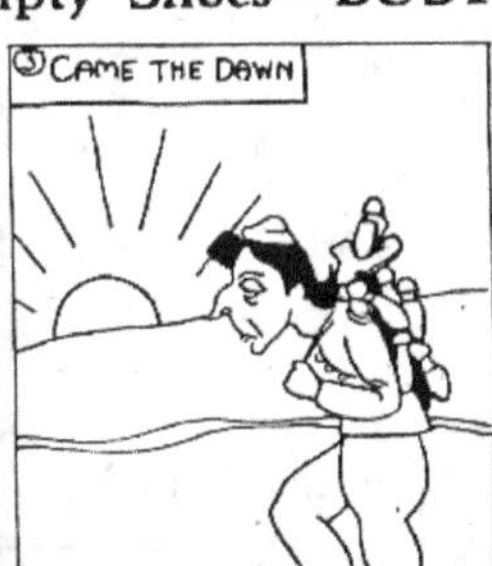

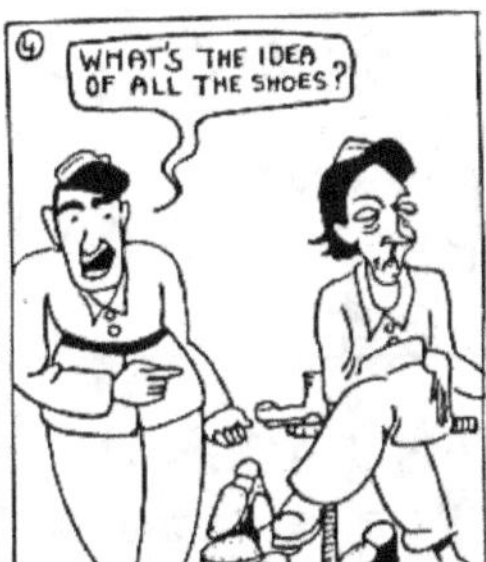

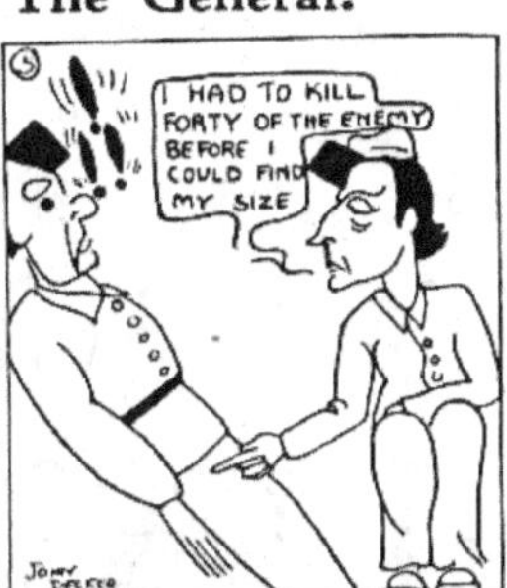

"LITTLE FROZEN FACE"—So This is War!—BUSTER KEATON in "The General."

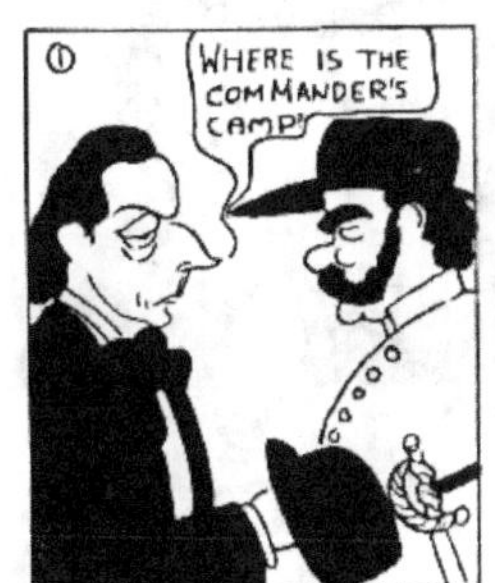

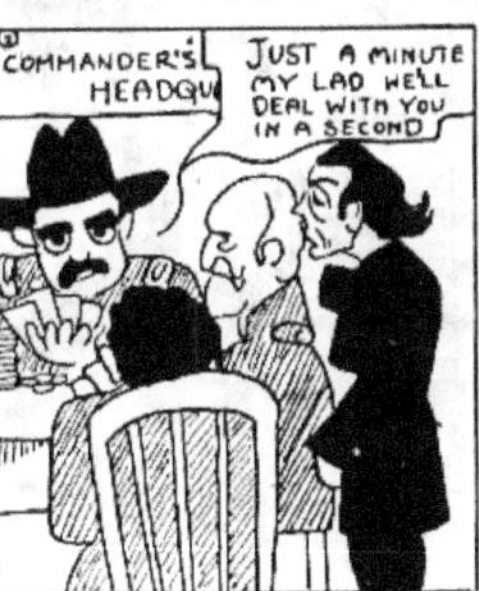

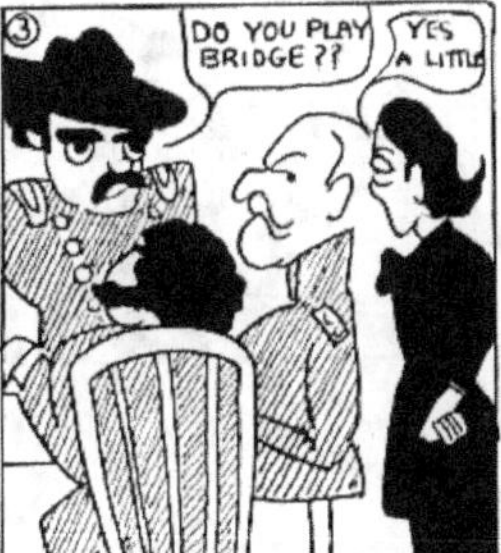

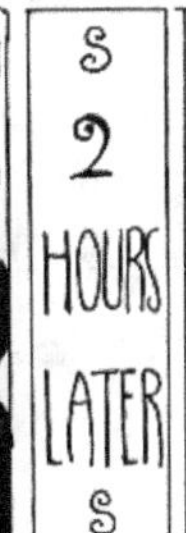

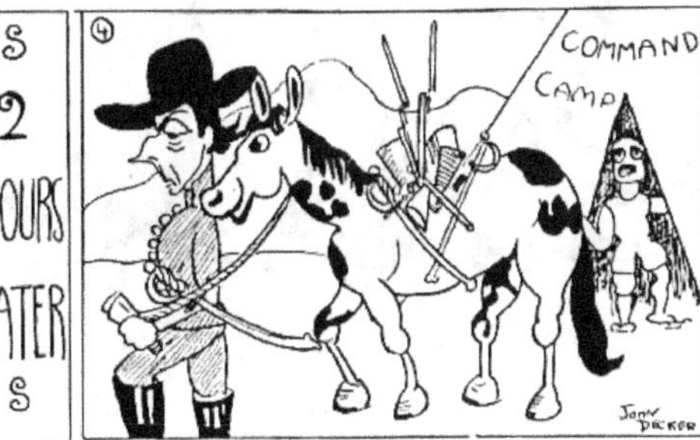

TIE-UPS AND CARTOONS

"LITTLE FROZEN FACE"—A Human Bullseye—BUSTER KEATON in "The General."

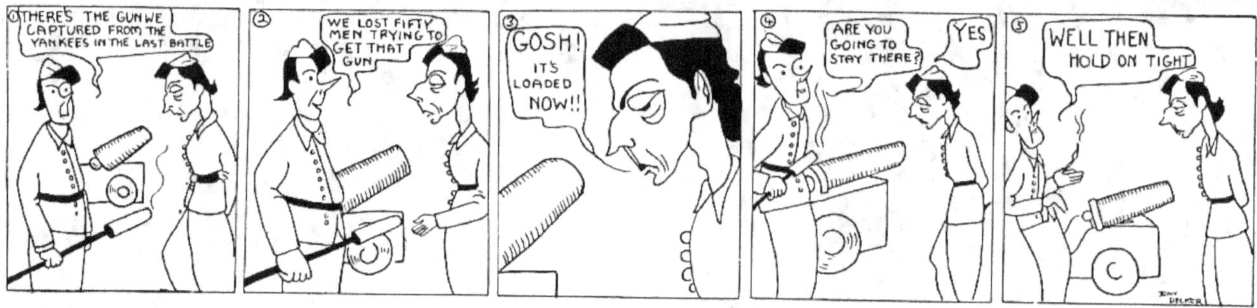

"LITTLE FROZEN FACE"—Not So Dumb—BUSTER KEATON in "The General."

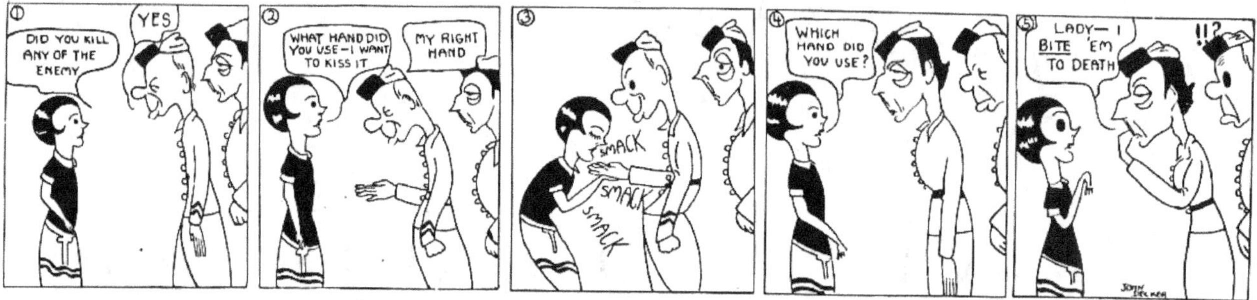

"LITTLE FROZEN FACE"—Wanted: An Ear Trumpet!—BUSTER KEATON in "The General."

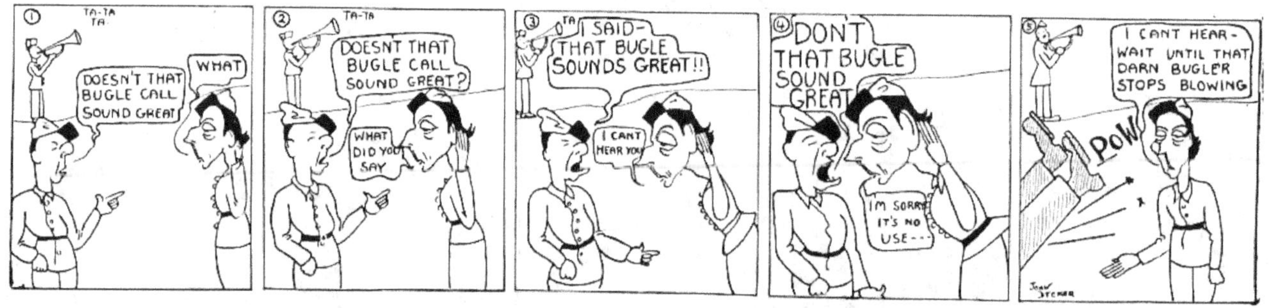

"LITTLE FROZEN FACE"—High Pressure—BUSTER KEATON in "The General."

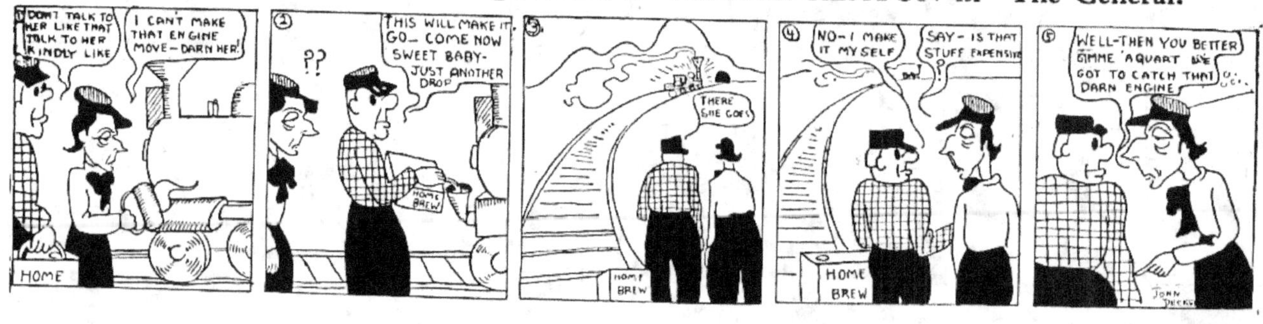

USE LOBBY NOVELTIES

Make up this old-time railroad table, suiting the hours to your performance schedule, and post it in lobby, around town, in railroad terminals,—anywhere it can be seen. For program or publicity use the cut is available. Get BKX—Two-Col. Time Table (Cut 50c; Mat 10c).

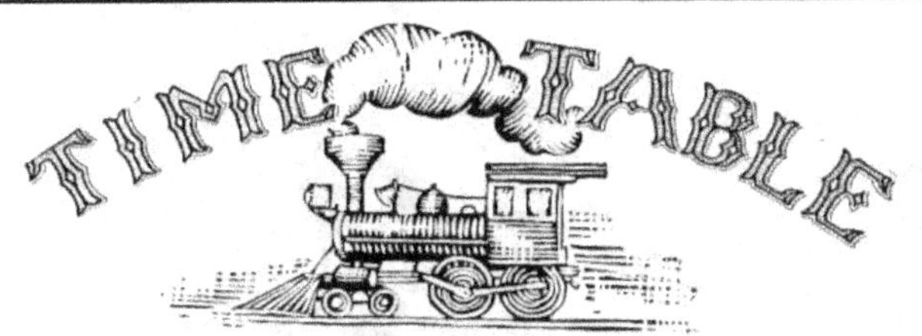

M. & A. R. R.—MAIN LINE STATION
BUSTER KEATON in "THE GENERAL"

Departure of Trains		Destinations
No. 11.	2:20 P.M.	*Smile Junction and Way Points.
		(Buster Keaton jilted at the roundhouse.)
No. 3.	2:24 P.M.	†Snickerville, via Grin Station.
		(Adopts locomotive as substitute sweetheart.)
No. 19.	2:31 P.M.	‡Shock, via Surprise.
		(Enemy steals locomotive and girl.)
No. 7.	2:36 P.M.	Clamor and Indignation.
		(Chases stolen engine on velocipede.)
No. 15.	2:41 P.M.	‖Laugh Ripples.
		(Switches to handcar.)
No. 1.	2:45 P.M.	Guffaws, Big Chuckles and Snorts.
		(Commandeers another engine.)
No. 5.	2:56 P.M.	Cheers, Gasps and all Way Points.
		(Continues chase over burning bridges.)
No. 13.	3:02 P.M.	§Conniption, Hysterics and all points North.
		(Spectacular collisions.)
No. 9.	3:11 P.M.	¶Howitzer, Seven Pines, and Shell Shriek.
		(Blunders into midst of red hot battle.)
No. 23.	3:20 P.M.	$Laugh Center, Climax Crossing and Daredevil, via Dumb Luck.
		(Buster and girl snared by foe.)
No. 17.	3:30 P.M.	Fun Riot.
		(Buster and girl break guardhouse.)
No. 13½.	3:36 P.M.	?Screams, Thrill, Panic and Chase.
		(Buster recaptures "The General.")
No. 21.	3:42 P.M.	Laughter, Runs Wild, and Way Stations.
		(Buster absorbs shock of enemy's rolling stock.)
No. 29.	3:48 P.M.	bHilarity, via Thrill.
		(Buster proves unknown hero.)
No. 33.	3:52 P.M.	Audience, Rolling-Off, Seats.
		(Buster wins war and joins army.)
No. 31.	3:58 P.M.	Huzzas, via Big Climax.
		(Buster wins girl.)

*Will not run except on Tuesdays, Wednesdays, Thursdays, Fridays, Saturdays, Sundays and Mondays.
†Mixed train.
¶Sherman was right.
?De luxe—carries cuspidors in day coach.

‡Daily except weekly.
‖Stops only on signal, and seldom then.
§Carries caboose.
bWill not run Feb. 30 nor June 31.

Each Picture Sold Individually on Merit

TRACKS

Lay sections of compo-board through your lobby and paint it as with tracks and ties—have the audience "walk the track" through the foyer.

You can make a startling effect with a short length of raised track in the lobby to the front of a locomotive appearing to come out of the wall.

SAFETY FIRST

Place three stacked guns in the lobby, a cork in each muzzle, and a placard:

These guns were loaded with laughter by Buster Keaton in "The General." The corks are to keep them from going off in the lobby. Step inside and hear the laugh bombardment.

JOSEPH M. SCHENCK
presents

BUSTER KEATON

in

"THE GENERAL"

UNITED ARTISTS PICTURE

UNITED ARTISTS CORPORATION

CONVULSING CATCH LINES

See "THE GENERAL" and surrender —to laughter.

———

Sherman said only half of it. War can be a frolic. See Buster Keaton in "THE GENERAL."

———

When Buster climbs into the cab, laughter has the right of way.

———

"THE GENERAL" — Biggest Keaton Komedy Ever Made—Buster's Most Hilarious Achievement!

———

He's in the army now! Buster Keaton as "THE GENERAL" leads the host of Joy against an army of Glooms.

———

Buster Keaton in "THE GENERAL" shows 'em how to run a war at 60 miles an hour!

———

A vast dramatic cataclysm convulsed with Buster Keaton's capers.

———

The North and the South united in a guffaw!

———

Scores of big scenes—
Hundreds of Thrills!
Thousands of soldiers!
Millions of Laughs!

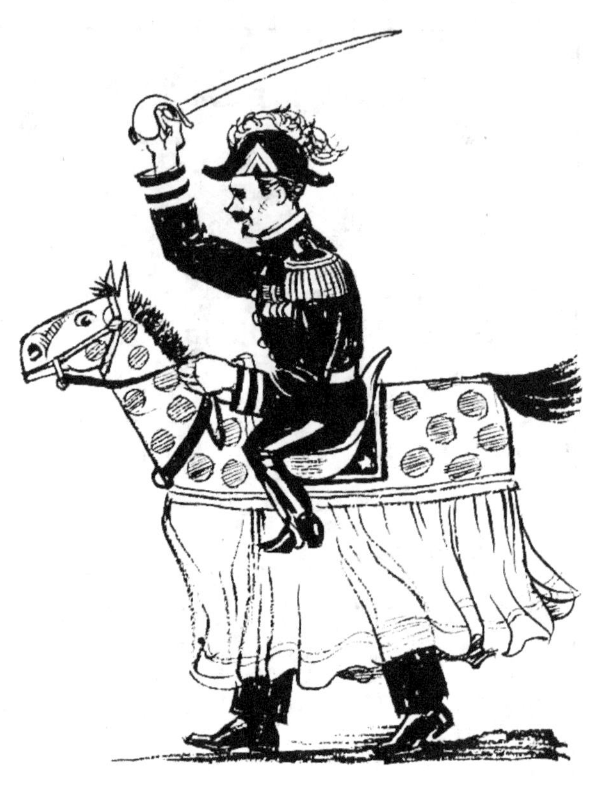

The Grays (alias Buster Keaton) driving away the Blues—and the Blues glad of it!

———

A comedy of undreamed-of magnitude and glamor.

———

"THE GENERAL"—the world's most decisive victory over Gloom!

CONVULSING CATCH LINES

Here comes "THE GENERAL"
Headin' down the line—
Runnin' slap-bang into an
OPEN SWITCH of HOWLS and
ROARS and LAUGHS!

A superb Comedy Spectacle of Laughs and Thrills!

Not a burlesque of the Civil War but a rip-roaring COMEDY of the period.

"THE GENERAL" is a choo-choo
That wanders far and near;
It's a joke to everybody—
Except its engineer.

Ludicrous railroading in the Sixties with Buster Keaton at the throttle.

Battles, bombardments, box cars and BUSTER KEATON!

"THE GENERAL"—tearing down an open track with a feather to tickle you in the ribs!

Frozen-faced Buster Keaton makes even the army mules laugh with "The General," the world's biggest laughtermotive engine!

"THE GENERAL"—the world's most decisive victory over Gloom!

A laugh feature on an unprecedented scale.

HOBBY HORSE

For a ballyhoo or for a stage presentation on the comedy order have a man represent "The General" on horseback with a hobby-horse outfit in which the man walks about in a frame representing a steed. Always good for a laugh.

KID WHISTLES

Get your young friends lined up through a distribution of "locomotive whistles." Any toy whistle will serve the purpose. This is a great aid toward working up special performances of "The General." Tag these whistles: "Toot! Toot! Here comes Buster Keaton in 'The General'—Regent Theatre."

The lighter side of war and railroading —Buster Keaton in "THE GENERAL."

Napoleon was right—an army marches on its stomach and laughs up its sleeve, as proved by Buster Keaton in his big comedy spectacle, "THE GENERAL."

The struggle between the States dramatized into a battle between locomotives with Buster Keaton as the wrecking crew.

CONVULSING CATCH LINES

A melange of mistakes, massed troops, medieval motive power and modern MIRTH.

———

Dramatic moments and madcap love vie with laughs throughout the story.

———

If you don't laugh yourself weak and get thrilled into gooseflesh while watching "THE GENERAL," you'd not even grin at Julius Caesar crossing the Alps on a high wheel bike.

———

A laugh and thrill riot from the opening flash to the final fadeout.

Heaps of handcars!
Blocks of boxcars!
Legions of locomotives!
The North—the South—
The Georgia belle—and—
BUSTER KEATON!

———

A vast dramatic cataclysm convulsed with Buster Keaton's capers.

———

The North and the South united in a guffaw!

———

Scores of big scenes—
Hundreds of Thrills!
Thousands of soldiers!
Millions of Laughs!

———

The Grays (alias Buster Keaton) driving away the Blues—and the Blues glad of it!

———

A comedy of undreamed-of magnitude and glamor.

———

"THE GENERAL"—the world's most decisive victory over Gloom!

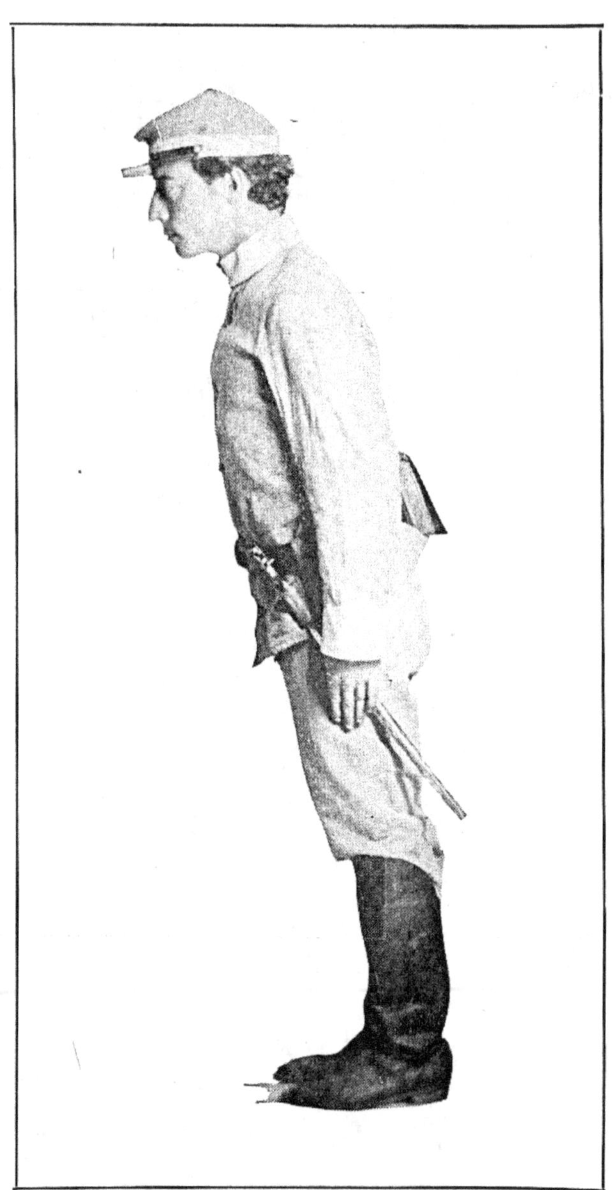

WAX WORKS

Fasten a pair of boots to the floor; have a man dressed as Keaton stand in the boots and lean forward at a precarious angle. Let him hold this position long at a time and perfectly immovable and expressionless. The idea is—"Is he alive?" Lots of talk is caused by this sort of stunt.

USE LOBBY NOVELTIES

"GENERAL" MDSE.

Don't overlook the opportunity for a big local tie-up with business concerns that operate under the title of General. Every city directory will give you a list of "General" establishments—from a hand laundry to the General Motors Company. Here is fine field for window or other tie-ups individually arranged. Or your newspaper may go after an advertising double truck by lining up most of the "General" firms for ad space round your theatre ad.

OTHER TIE-UPS

BICYCLES.—Get a sporting goods store window display centered round a wooden high-wheeled bike, like Buster's, in contrast with modern stock. (See Still No. 218.)

OIL CANS.—Hardware stores will see an excuse in Still No. 3 and others to feature a display of oil cans and monkey wrenches.

QUILTS.—Get antique shops and women's exchanges to display log cabin quilts of the civil war period. (See Still No. 182.) There is also a contest idea in this.

CLOTHING.—A good idea for a special clothing store attention display is seen in two wax figures representing Buster Keaton shaking hands with himself—on one side as a Union and on the other as a Confederate soldier.

OVERALLS.—Have a dealer stage a window display with a draped set of overalls, using a cut-out head of Buster Keaton to complete the figure to represent him as the engineer of "The General." There's plenty of poster material for cut-outs.

ARMY STORES.—This is an especially appropriate tie-up. There's no end of appropriate material for an army store window.

FURNITURE. — Have a department store put in an 1862 window, with an old time loan collection of furniture to contrast with more modern wares.

TOYS.—Suggest to a toy dealer that he make over one of his electric toy trains into a train of 1862 by slipping a pasteboard funnel smoke stack on it and masking a few other parts with pasteboard alterations until it resembles "The General." There's also a lobby display idea here.

UTILIZE THESE SIX-DAY TEASER ADS:

GENERAL Pershing may have four stars, but this "GENERAL" has only one star—Buster Keaton!

(Your Theatre)—Next Week

France had a GENERAL in Napoleon, but "The GENERAL" has a Napoleon in Buster Keaton.

(Your Theatre)—Next Week

GENERAL Wellington won at Waterloo, but Buster Keaton's "GENERAL" won at water too.

(Your Theatre)—Next Week

GENERAL Delivery gives you your mail, but Buster Keaton's GENERAL delivers your Mirth.

(Your Theatre)—Next Week

Fabius was a Roman GENERAL, but you ought to see "The GENERAL" roamin' with Buster Keaton.

(Your Theatre)—Next Week

"Give 'em more grape!" cried the GENERAL to the Captain.
"Give 'em more laughs!" cried Private Buster Keaton to "The GENERAL."

(Your Theatre)—Next Week

MAIL AND PROGRAM IDEAS

SELL LAUGHS BY DIRECT MAIL:

Aboard "THE GENERAL"
Laughter Unlimited

Dear Patron:

If ever you receive a sincere invitation to laugh to the limit, this is it!

Buster Keaton in the biggest comedy he has ever made -- biggest in action, in thrills, in wit, humor and downright swirls of joy -- is coming to the -------- Theatre next week.

"The General" is the hilarious adventure of an oldtime wood burner locomotive and a frozen faced engineer. It has the most laughs, thrills and breakneck love ever crammed into a motion picture. A huge panorama of a period when engines had pet names instead of Pullman cars.

LOVE, LOCOMOTIVES and LAUGHS!

Get ready for some of those rich, rare riots of MIRTH!

Here comes "THE GENERAL" with Buster at the throttle!

Yours merrily,

Manager.

PROGRAM COPY

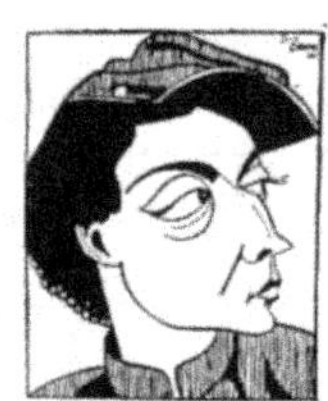

For this cut order BK-O (Electro only; Price 20 cents)

Come on aboard! Take a hair-raising, side-splitting excursion with Buster Keaton in "The GENERAL"!

Get the gasps that Buster Keaton gets at the throttle of an old-time, wood-burner locomotive, as he rockets back and forth across battle lines, over bridges and into tunnels to save his pet engine and his sweetheart.

Take a front seat with the love-sick locomotive engineer blissfully booming through a million hazards!

Get your tickets at the box office of the Regent Theatre! Come early to avoid having to stand up while we go round the curves! You'll

LAUGH

THRILL

LAUGH

at Buster Keaton in "The GENERAL"—a dynamic upheaval of boxcars, bombardments and breathless blunders!

SHOWMANSHIP HELPS

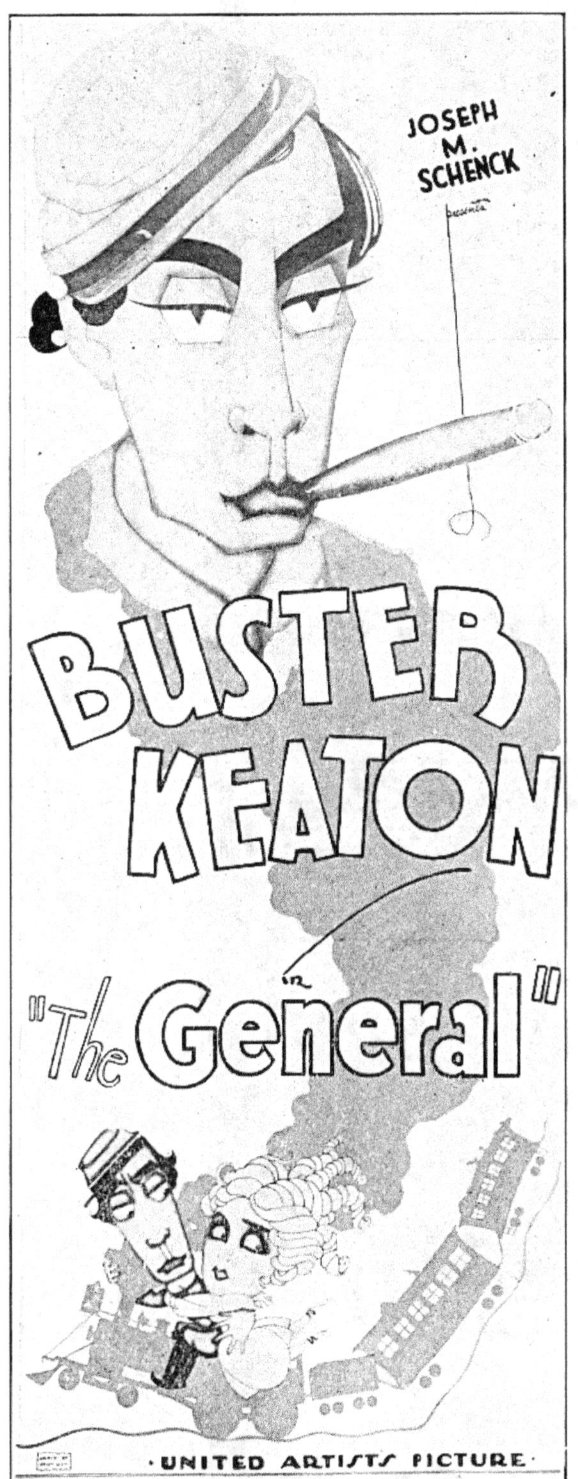

MUSIC CUES

Ask for music cues on Buster Keaton in "The General" at any United Artists Corporation exchange.

An especially effective musical accompaniment has been arranged for this elaborate comedy production, with themes calculated to emphasize every thrill and laugh episode.

INSERT CARD

At the left is illustrated the insert card on Buster Keaton in "The General," another attractive sample of the new series of United Artists Corporation accessories. This insert card is hand-colored and comes in the regulation 14 x 36 size for use in insert frames.

Price 25 cents each; or 20 cents each in quantities over fifty. Order from the exchange.

TRAILERS

Authorized trailers on Joseph M. Schenck's presentation of Buster Keaton in "The General" may be obtained from the

National Screen Service, Inc.

Order direct from National Screen Service, Inc., at one of the following headquarters:

NEW YORK—
126 West 46th Street.

CHICAGO—
845 South Wabash Avenue.

LOS ANGELES—
1922 South Vermont Avenue.

(Do not order from United Artists Corporation.)

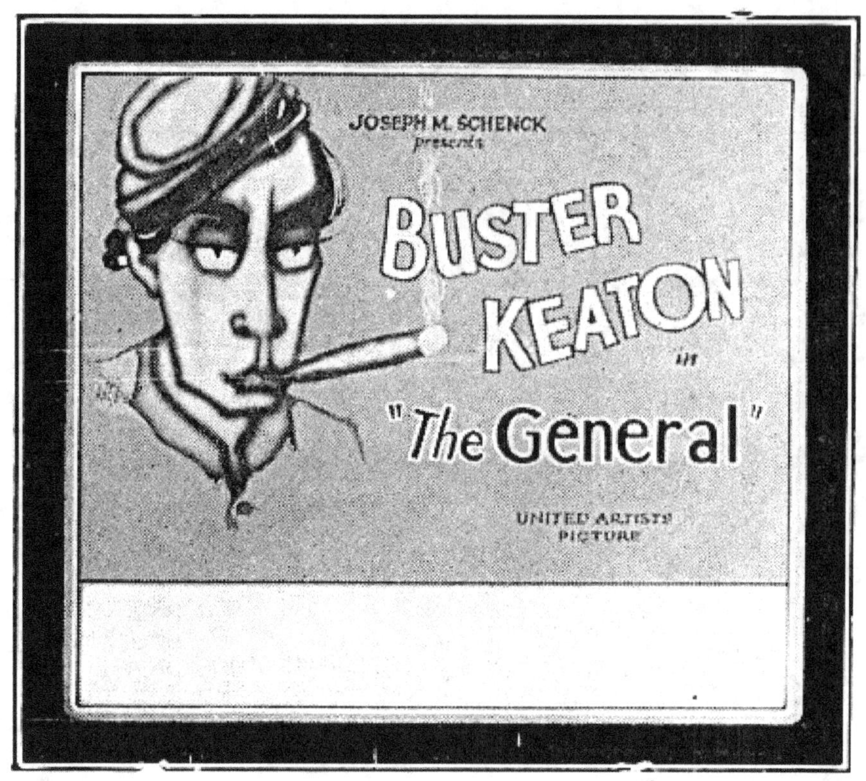

Slide No. 1 (Price 15 Cents)

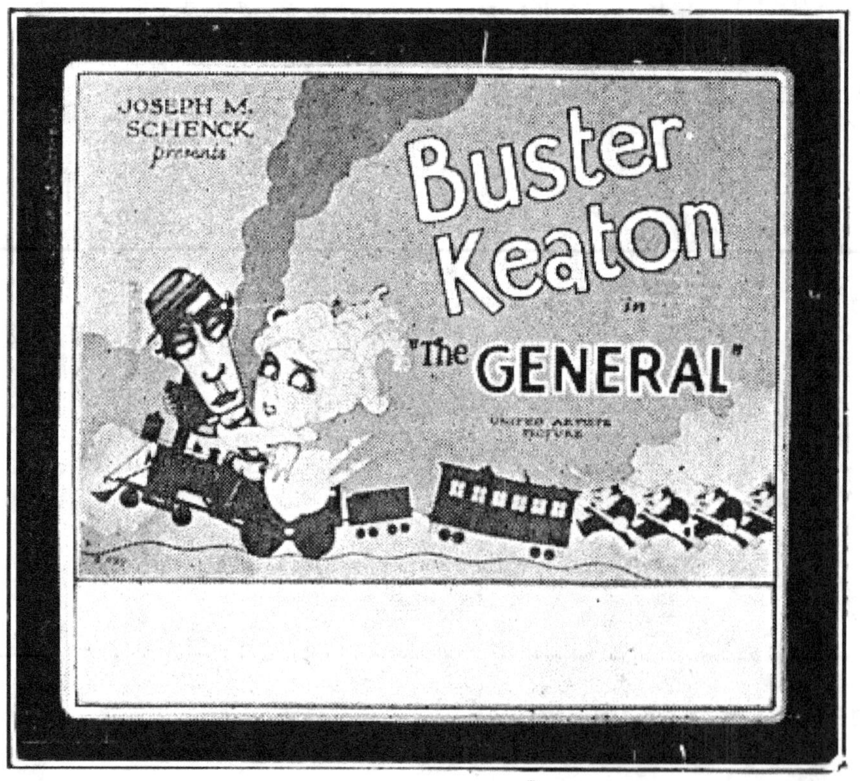

Slide No. 2 (Price 15 Cents)

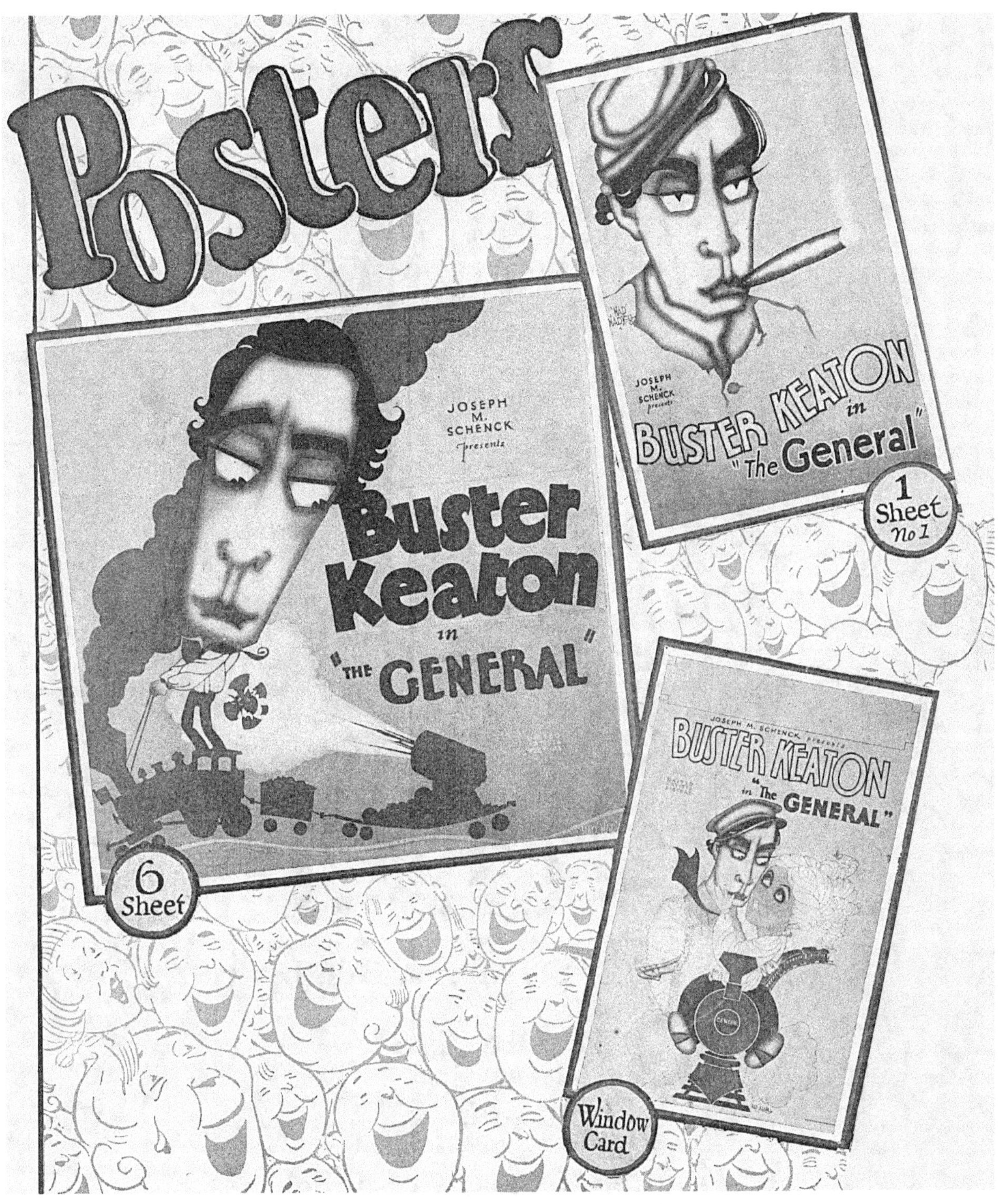
Posters

JOSEPH M. SCHENCK presents

BUSTER KEATON
in "The General"

1 Sheet No 1

JOSEPH M. SCHENCK presents

BUSTER KEATON
in "THE GENERAL"

6 Sheet

JOSEPH M. SCHENCK presents

BUSTER KEATON
in "THE GENERAL"

Window Card

Showman's Campaign Book

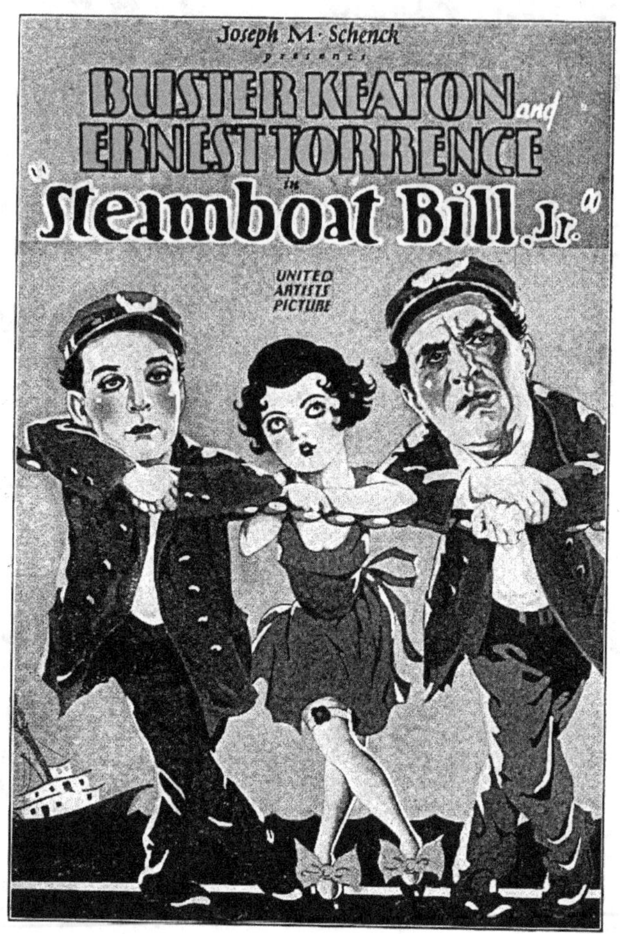

Buster Keaton's "Steamboat Bill, Jr." (1928)

Feature Film

71 Minutes

Original Release Pressbook

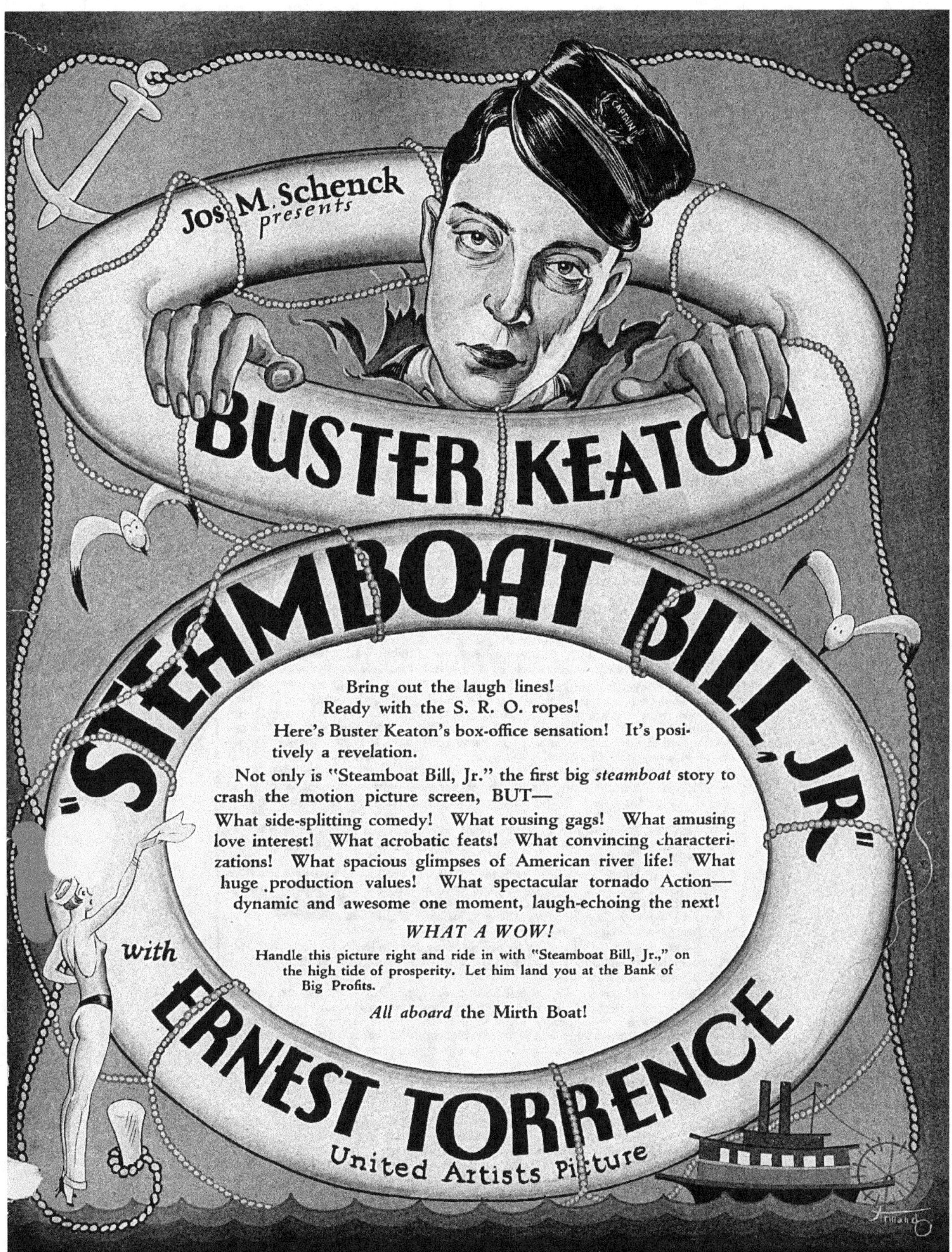

Give Your Audience a Big-Time Screamboat Joy Ride!

JOSEPH M. SCHENCK
presents
BUSTER KEATON AND ERNEST TORRENCE
in
"STEAMBOAT BILL, JR."
United Artists Picture

Directed by Charles F. Reisner

Story by Carl Harbaugh

Photographed by Dev Jennings and Bert Haines

Technical Director, Fred Gabourie

Assistant Director, Sandy Roth

CAST

Steamboat Bill	Ernest Torrence
His First Mate	Tom Lewis
Mr. King, His Rival	Tom McGuire
Mary King, His Daughter	Marion Byron
Steamboat Bill, Jr.	Buster Keaton

THE STORY.

A sleepy river town on the lower Mississippi has suddenly awakened and is staging the biggest celebration in its history.

Buildings are gaily decorated; the levee is in holiday attire; people are massed along the river bank; a band is blaring martial tunes; everybody seems to be happy.

All but one person—"Steamboat Bill," owner of the packet "Stonewall Jackson".

The occasion for the celebration is the arrival of a new boat which henceforth is to ply between River Junction and southern ports. And the owner of "The King" is letting the townspeople know that he is out to run "Steamboat Bill" off the river. King, who has modestly named his craft after himself, has practically secured control of the town.

Bill used to be the "leading citizen", but by lavish expenditures and much smooth talk about what he's going to do for River Junction, King, a newcomer in the state, has prejudiced the citizens and convinced them that the veteran steamboater and his antiquated boat are dangerous.

A few days later Bill receives good news; his son, whom he hasn't seen since babyhood—the mother, since dead, having taken the child to Boston to rear in a different environment than "that rough river town"—is scheduled to arrive to live with his father. Bill decides that with his husky son to aid him, he'll be able to prevent King and the rich man's crowd from ruining him financially. Bill himself is six foot, three inches tall, and he hopes the boy, now grown to manhood, will be at least six feet four.

When Bill's offspring arrives, however, the giant steamboat pilot gets the shock of his life. Young Bill is a shrimp, wears college clothes, plays a ukulele and rolls his r's.

Nothing daunted, Bill reflects that after all, a son is a son, so he sneaks him up an alley, gets him into some he-man clothes, and tries to make a river man out of him.

The ruthless river war continues. Steamboat Bill is being gradually a rabbit in a lion's den, but if nothing else, he's game, loyal to his father, and a glutton for punishment. He is also susceptible to feminine charms, for the minute he meets Mary King, daughter of his father's bitter rival, he's head over heels in love.

The romance of the couple proceeds under difficulties; their fathers discover the affair and forbid further meetings, with the result they are forced to exchange vows clandestinely.

The ruthless river war continues. Steamboat Bill is being gradually forced to the wall by King and his more powerful organization when an opportunity arises for a coup which will restore the veteran to his former prestige. Bill Junior throws the proverbial monkey-wrench into the plans, and the father is so disgusted with his seemingly worthless son that he orders the youth back to Boston.

Bill Junior leaves, but returns to River Junction in the dead of night and discovers that his father has been jailed for getting into a fist-fight with King. The youth hoodwinks the jailer, smuggles his father out of a cell and, again reconciled, continues the war with his father against King.

Discovering some of King's henchmen in the act of attempting to wreck the "Stonewall Jackson", Bill and his son give battle, with the result that the father is returned to jail, and Junior, injured, is sent to a hospital. Mary, estranged from her sweetheart because of the family feud, refuses to visit him.

King's triumph is shortlived; a tornado hits River Junction; all the boats but Bill's are swept from their moorings, and the townspeople, driven from their homes by storm and flood, take refuge on the old "Stonewall Jackson". Young Bill forgets his hurts, escapes from the hospital and takes charge of the situation.

A real river man at last, Bill Junior rescues his father, pilots the tornado survivors to safety, and winds up in a blaze of glory by risking his life to save Mary.

Give Your Audience a Big-Time Screamboat Joy Ride!

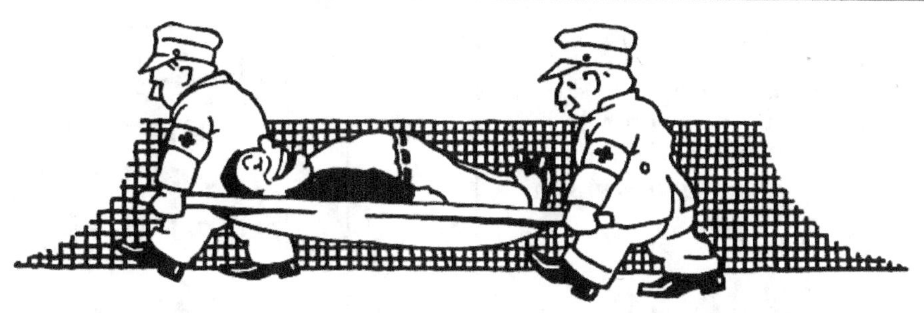

He Laughed Himself Well!

AND SO WILL YOU, IF YOU PINE
FOR MIRTH, WHEN YOU WITNESS

BUSTER KEATON *and*
ERNEST TORRENCE
in
"STEAMBOAT BILL, Jr."

at the RIALTO THEATRE (date)

Use this Cut For novelty ads. and for teaser throwaway. Order:
BLX-9—Two-Col. Stretcher Mat, 10c; cut, 30c.
Actual size of Cut, 3½ in. wide by 1⅛ in. high.

Pink Page

FOR special publicity do not overlook the pink sheet feature: "'STEAMBOAT BILL, Jr.,' Re-written as a Piece for the Third Reader," which is bound in pink paper as Page 11 of the Publicity Stories section of this Campaign Book. Obtain space for this unique humor stunt in the feature section of your newspaper, and use the special cut, BLX-10—Two-Col. Third Reader.

River Music

"STEAMBOAT BILL, JR.," offers a brilliant opportunity for musical offerings and presentations featuring such favorite melodies as "Swanee River," "On the Banks of the Wabash," "The Mississippi Shore," and similar numbers new and old, including a large number of "blues."

A Special Art Sketch

Here we have a character sketch of Buster Keaton in a Bushnell line drawing. Use it as a variation from halftone newspaper and program copy.

Order BLX-5—One-Col. Sketch Keaton
(Mat 5c; Cut 30c)

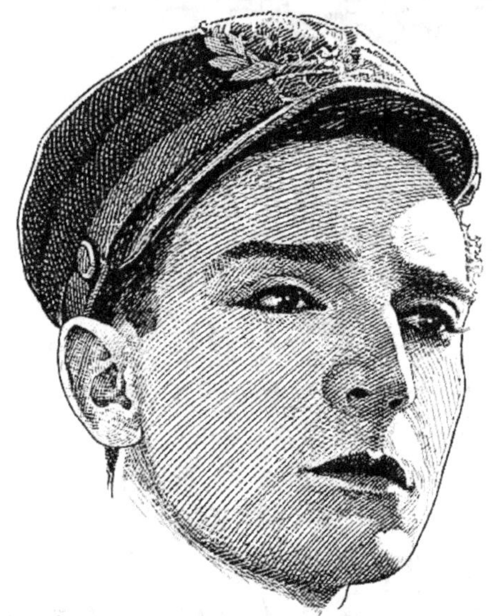

Buster Keaton in "STEAMBOAT BILL, JR"

(Actual size of cut: 2 in. wide by 3 in. high, including caption.)

Ushers

GIVE your men ushers natty double-breasted blue suits with brass buttons. Your girls should wear white double-breasted jackets and white skirts.

Frozen Face

ENGAGE a "smileless man" to pose in your lobby, dressed as Buster Keaton. Challenge your public to make "Steamboat Bill, Jr." laugh. Give a ticket of admission to each person who can do so. You can add interest by having him sit or stand in a pilot house built of compo board.

Order BLX-7d—One-Col. Laugh Teaser. (On Two-Col. Mat of Four, 10c; Cuts, each 30c.)

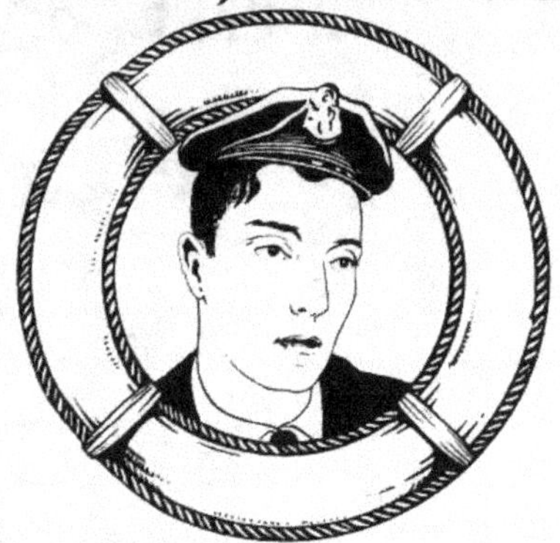

(The actual size of this cut is 2 in. wide by 4 in. high.)

Laugh Teasers

ON this spread are four One-Col. cuts for use as a Teaser Ad. seires, one to be published daily. They are designated BLX-a-b-c and d. They build up a progressive laugh idea for the production.

Note that the four BLX-7 Laugh Teasers are all on one special mat (Mat, 20c). The cuts come separately mounted, at 30c for each cut. Order cuts separately as BLX-7 a, b, c, and d.

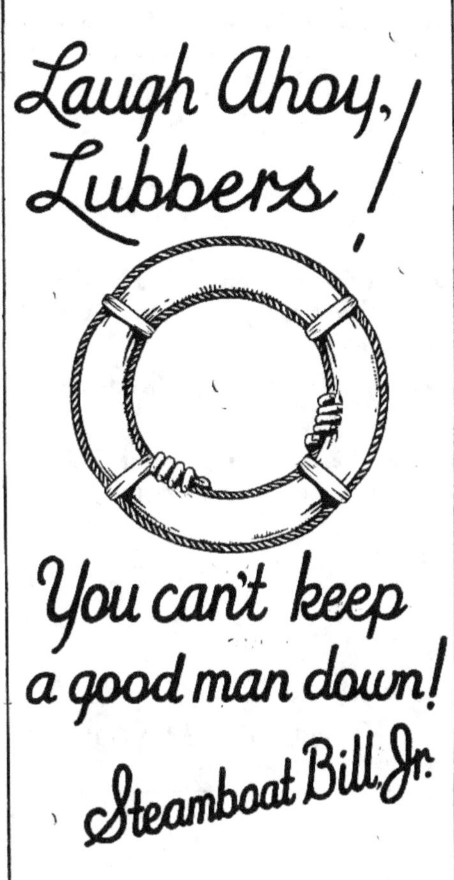

Order BLX-7b—One-Col. Laugh Teaser. (On Two-Col. Mat of Four, 10c; Cuts, each 30c.)

(The actual size of this cut is 2 in. wide by 4 in. high.)

Attracters

Place anchors painted in bright colors in front of your theatre. Placard them: "Buster Keaton and Ernest Torrence in their big river comedy, 'Steamboat Bill, Jr.', are anchored here. You can't miss it!"

Have Negroes dressed as roustabouts seated on cotton bales in your lobby or atop your marquee playing banjoes and singing.

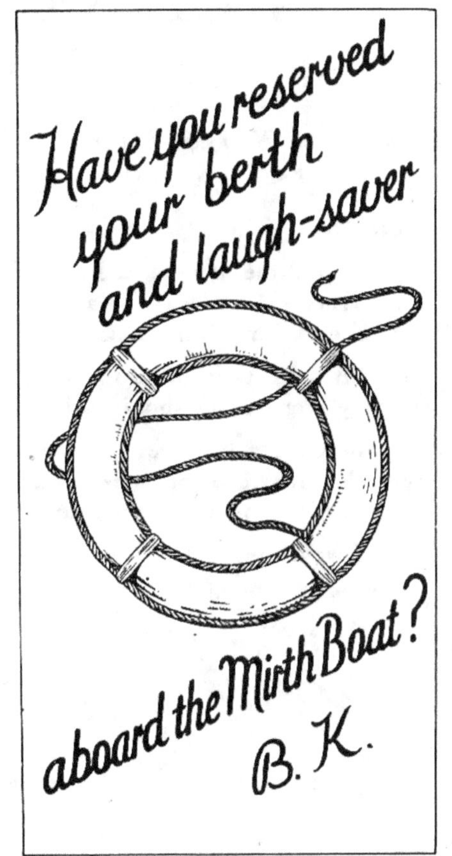

This is BLX-7a, on Two-Col. Mat of Four, with 7-b, c and d. (Mat of all, 10c; Cuts, each 30c.)

(The actual size of this cut is 2 in. wide by 4 in. high.)

Street Stuff

Run an auto or sidecar motorcycle through the streets with a reproduction of a steamboat pilot house mounted over the body. Use an appropriate "Steamboat Bill, Jr.," display billing.

Obtain a quantity of little white sailor hats such as are on sale at every 5 and 10 cent store. Have your artist letter them with "Steamboat Bill, Jr.," copy, and distribute them to street newsdealers or newsboys to wear during the run of the comedy.

"STEAMBOAT BILL, Jr."

(A LETTER)

MR. ERNEST TORRENCE,
Palooka City, Ark.

Dear Dad:

Expect me home at the end of this semester to help aboard the steamboat. It's now sixteen years since I've seen a river, and I'll wager Mrs. Sippi (Mississippi) — ha! ha! — missed me. But I'll introduce modern ideas once I get back to aqua firma.

Shall I get measured for a yachting cap and blue suit with brass buttons? I already have a riding crop, tennis shoes, and a ukulele.

Hope I may have shore leave ever and anon. I've met the Miss King whose father runs the other boat on your river. I dare say he and you, dear pater, are fast friends, even though his ship gets all the trade.

I want to take Miss King to see us all in "Steamboat Bill, Jr.," at the _______________
Theatre, beginning ______________. Miss King loves to laugh.

Au revoir—or, as they say in Mayfair, pip, pip!

Your devoted son,

BUSTER KEATON.

Model building contests are always good for a terrific response in the way of publicity, good will and box-office profits.

Start the contest for a "Steamboat Bill, Jr." model fully three weeks in advance of your opening. Give the boys a chance to make their steamboats, and give yourself a chance to capitalize on the contest.

Get newspaper cooperation and school cooperation, if possible. Get department store cooperation for a tremendous window display of competing models, just before your "Steamboat Bill, Jr." opens.

Offer worthwhile prizes—and also boost the contest on your screen.

You will have the whole town interested in a short time.

Boys, Build a "Steamboat Bill, Jr." Model !!

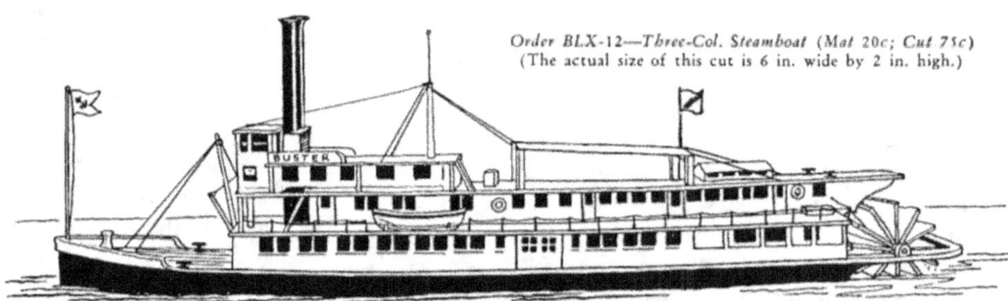

Order BLX-12—Three-Col. Steamboat (Mat 20c; Cut 75c)
(The actual size of this cut is 6 in. wide by 2 in. high.)

How many clever boys with tools have wondered what to make next? Well, here it is!
Get right to work and make a "Steamboat Bill, Jr." model steamboat!
Look at this picture and build a model resembling it. It is the Mississippi river craft upon which Buster Keaton, the famous comedian, and Ernest Torrence, noted character actor, have their side splitting adventures in the movie of "Steamboat Bill, Jr." which will soon be seen at the_________________
Theatre.
With the fun of making the model, you may win valuable prizes and a chance to see the show as well.
Make your model any size you please. Make it of wood, or tin or pasteboard. Change the design if you want to. The best looking models will win. Paint the superstructure white, the smoke stacks black, and the hull red.
(Other rules here.)
(List of prizes here.)

(FOR DESCRIPTION OF THESE ILLUSTRATIONS SEE PAGE FOUR)

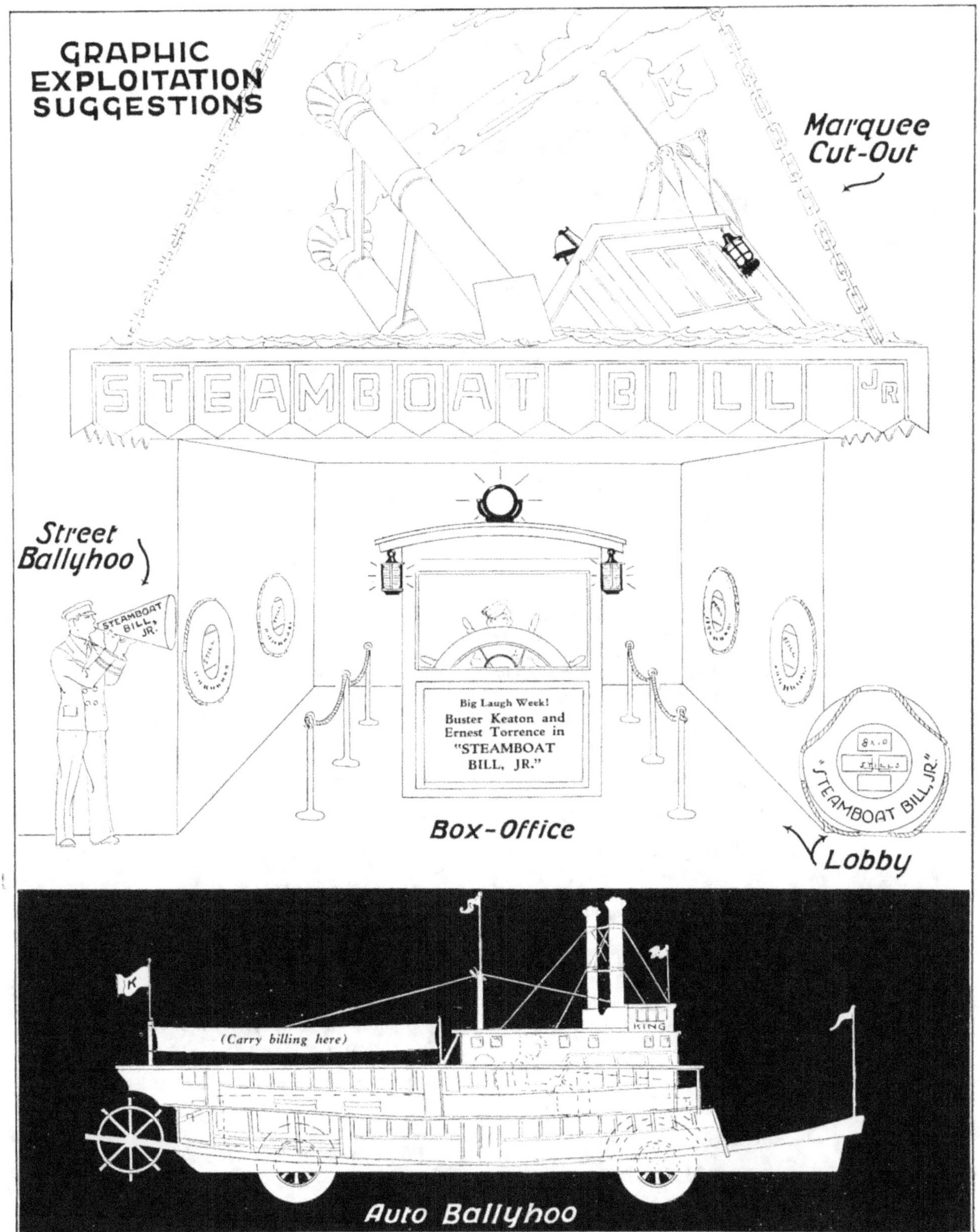

Joseph M. Schenck Presents

BUSTER KEATON and ERNEST TORRENCE in

"STEAMBOAT BILL, Jr."

United Artists Picture

Tie To These Exploitation Ideas:

Prize Ads.—In co-operation with literature, journalism and art classes of your local schools conduct a competition for the best advertising layout or poster heralding Buster Keaton and Ernest Torrence in "Steamboat Bill, Jr." at your theatre. Provide them with still pictures, portraits, billing, heralds and other material to work from. Be sure to inaugurate this contest at least two weeks in advance of your opening date. Plan to use the best specimens as reproductions in the newspapers and as an exhibition in your lobby or in a department store window.

Drawing Contest.—The idea of making Buster Keaton laugh is always a good one. Print BL-1, BL-2 or BLX-5 with Keaton's mouth tooled out, and offer awards to those persons who can draw in the best laughing mouth to complete the illustration.

Love Problem.—Conduct a letter writing contest on the topic:

"Would You Save A Girl From Drowning Who Had Jilted You?"

Laugh Lines.—Attach a short piece of slender hemp cord to a shipping tag. On the tag print:

A Laugh Line For You!

This is a piece of rope with which we will tie up with our boatload of laughs at the Rialto next Monday.

We know you'll like our line.

BUSTER KEATON *and*
ERNEST TORRENCE *in*

"Steamboat Bill, Jr."

Send quantities of these tags in envelopes to a restricted mailing list in advance of your showing.

Radio Stunt.—Sponsor a "Steamboat Bill, Jr." radio program, featuring steamboat songs, river songs, and so forth. Offer awards of tickets to listeners who can identify the largest list of the songs played.

Parodies.—Offer prizes in co-operation with a newspaper for the best parodied verse of the old song, "Steamboat Bill," tying up, of course, with your show.

Sailor Kids.—Proud parents have a fad of dressing five-year-old tots in naval costume. Set a date on which you will admit free all children under a certain age who come wearing sailor or yachting suits. Take a picture of them in a group and offer it to your newspaper.

Teaser Copy

It won't be long now!
The funniest BILL in the world is coming!

———

Jest wait!
"Steamboat Bill, Jr.," will take you floatin' down the river of Mirth in the laffinest picture made!

———

The (name of Theatre) presents its funniest comedy BILL.

———

Hear dat whistle round dat bend?
"STEAMBOAT BILL, JR.'S" "comin' !"

Merchant Co-operation

DOUBLE TRUCK AD—Arrange with local firms for a co-operative double truck ad. in a newspaper, featuring the "Junior" idea. Get firms like "Thomas Jones, Jr., Co., Inc.," and, in fact, any firms that have a "Jr." in their title, to take space. The newspaper advertising manager will take hold of the idea.

TOYS—Get toy steamboats and steamships featured in shop windows, with still pictures to tie up with the "Steamboat Bill, Jr." comedy.

NAUTICAL GOODS—Obtain window displays of field glasses, telescopes, compasses, and similar articles in optical goods stores; also of nautical articles in ship chandlers' stores.

CLOTHING—Obtain window displays in clothing stores. Use models of "Bill, Jr." in his dress uniform and in his "sloppy weather" attire as contrasts for a "clothes make the man" idea. Use stills from "Steamboat Bill, Jr." to embellish the windows, and a slogan: "They laugh at Buster

Keaton on the screen and they'll laugh at you on the street if you don't dress up."

HATS—Use the hat fitting stills from "Steamboat Bill, Jr." for a tie up in hat store windows. Use a card: "Buster Keaton in 'Steamboat Bill, Jr.' at the Rialto can't find a hat to fit, but here anybody can."

BARBERS—Use stills of Buster and the girl in barber chairs for a tonsorial tie-up captioned: "When a screen star visits the barber."

NECKTIES—Use the still showing the girl tying Buster's new tie, for a haberdasher's display.

BALLYHOOS MARQUEE LOBBY

(For illustrations see full page drawing on page 5 opposite. No cuts nor mats).

MARQUEE—A painted beaver board cut-out of sunken steamer. Use a practical lantern, bell and flag, and have smoke drifting from the stacks at intervals, also sound bell and whistle at intervals . . . . Another marquee would have the upright pilot house and stacks. A man with megaphone atop the structure could cry out "All aboard for the mirth boat, 'Steamboat Bill, Jr.'"

LOBBY—Beaver board cut-outs to represent life preservers trimmed with real ropes and used as frames to display scene stills or 11 x 14 lobby cards.

BOX OFFICE—Booth enclosed in painted beaver board representing the pilot house. Green and red ship lanterns, lighted, at the sides; a spot as searchlight above. . . . . Where it is feasible, have a gangplank leading to the auditorium entrance.

STREET WORK—A man in natty captain's attire using a megaphone to announce the attraction.

AUTO SHIP — Painted beaver board enclosure or cut-out mounted on a chassis or a truck. Title of the attraction carried on a banner. A smoke pot to provide smoke for the stacks. Flags and lights may also be used. Also the paddle wheel may be made to operate.

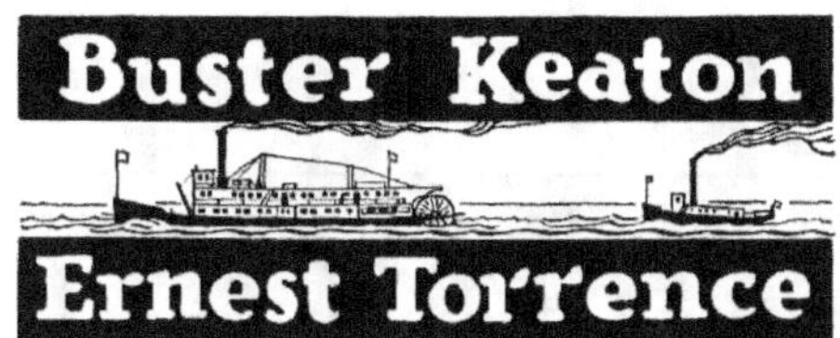

Program Copy:

HAVE you ever seen a gala day in a river town when the whole population dressed in its best, trooped down to the city wharf to welcome a flag-bedecked floating palace, its deep whistle and its yodeling calliope vieing with the cheers of the multitude?

Well, just like that, the whole town will throng to the Rialto Theatre next week, when the world's merriest, biggest and, in fact, its first Mississippi river comedy, "Steamboat Bill, Jr.", makes its advent.

ith Buster Keaton in the pilot hous ! The navigatin'est navigator that ever navigated!

And Ernest Torrence as Captain Bill, Sr., the most humanly convincing river character of present or modern times!

And Marion Byron, as a flapper heroine who has not only It, but That and Those!

And a performing troupe of big and little steamboats, tornadoes, floods, Main streets, and thrills in the skies overhead and on the earth and in the waters beneath!

Boys, this is Buster's biggest. Girls, this is a gigglefest to tell your grandchildren of!

Buster Keaton — in "Steamboat Bill, Jr." with Ernest Torrence!

(Use copy like the above for your program with Cut BL-1 or BLX-5.)

Work the River

RIVER towns are especially happy in playing "Steamboat Bill, Jr.", and the river situation should be played up to the limit.

Tie in with a steamboat company for a spectacular delivery of the film, with flags flying, bands playing, and a parade from the wharf.

Have Steamboatmen's Night, at which the old timers of the river traffic will be guests of honor . . . mates, captains, pilots and steamboat magnates. Get interviews with old river men for newspaper anecdotes.

Placard all steamboat landings above and below town.

KEATON'S NOSE BROKEN IN MAKING PICTURE

An unscheduled steamboat collision, an accident that cost Buster Keaton a broken nose, and other mishaps failed to interfere with the filming of the frozen-faced star's new United Artists feature, "Steamboat Bill Jr.," which will be shown at the .... Theatre starting ....

The company spent two months at a made-to-order river town across from Sacramento, the California state capital, and then worked for several weeks in Hollywood, filming interior scenes

Keaton, whose motion picture career has been marked by broken bones ever since he played minor roles in two-reelers, ran true to form during the filming of "Steamboat Bill Jr." when his nose came in contact with a baseball hurled by a member of a Sacramento team. Keaton's own nine, which he always takes with him on location, was playing another amateur organization when the accident occurred. Buster could not appear before the camera in close-ups for several days.

Two of the steamboats chartered by the Keaton company crashed without doing serious damage. Keaton, Ernest Torrence, who is playing a straight comedy role, and Marion Byron, who has the leading feminine part in "Steamboat Bill Jr.," were enacting a scene when the craft came together.

Charles "Chuck" Reisner, director, and Harry Brand, general manager of the Keaton company, averted an incipient panic among hundreds of extras.

"Steamboat Bill Jr.," an original story by Keaton's scenario staff, of which Carl Harbaugh is the head, is the comedy star's third United Artists feature, the others being "The General" and "College".

Buster Keaton, who is now appearing in "Steamboat Bill, Jr.," participated in the late World War. He was detailed to entertain the troops on the other side after the Armistice had been signed, and remained abroad for five months after hostilities had ceased.

A cyclone is the finale of "Steamboat Bill, Jr.," the United Artists picture in which Buster Keaton and Ernest Torrence are to be seen at the .... theatre. These sequences cost $255,000 to film and they are said to represent the most costly comedy scenes in any Keaton film

"STEAMBOAT BILL, Jr."

HERE is a novel contest that will prove itself a winner.

Use the accompanying illustration:

¶ Have a newspaper run the cut with plenty of white space above it, to allow of a hat being drawn in by contestants.

¶ Print rules of the contest under the coupon. The coupon is to be filled out with the name and address of the contestant, and is to be sent in to the newspaper along with the finished sketch.

¶ Use prizes of cash or of theatre tickets.

¶ You can get local hatters to co-operate with offers of a man's hat as the first prize.

¶ You can even use the cut and contest as the center of a co-operative page in which local hat dealers take space, each one offering a prize for the best hat sketch sent in by their own customers.

¶ In case a tie-up with a newspaper is not effected, the contest can be conducted directly by the theatre printing the cut on cards distributed to patrons the week before "Steamboat Bill, Jr." opens.

Put a Hat on "Steamboat Bill, Jr."

Order BLX-8—Two-Col. Hat Contest (Mat 10c, Cut 50c.)

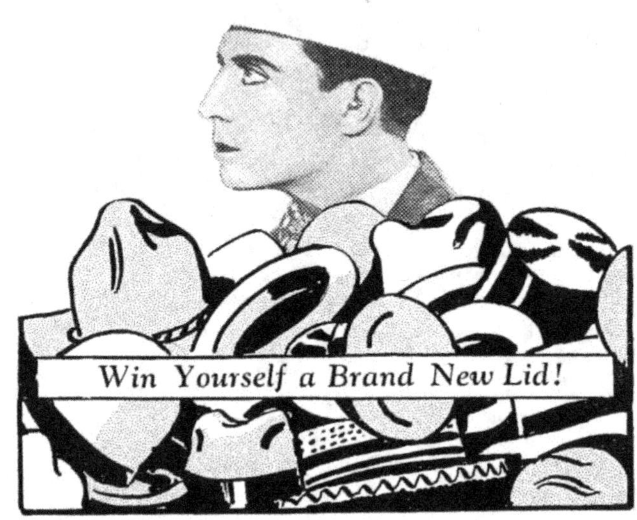

Actual size of Mat or Cut 4 in. wide, 3½ in. high.

"Steamboat Bill, Jr." Editor,
    Daily Enterprise.

    The hat on the above sketch of Buster Keaton in "Steamboat Bill, Jr." coming to the Rialto Theatre next week, was drawn by the undersigned:

Name ________________________________

Address ________________________________

My favorite local hatter is ________________________________

"Steamboat Bill, Jr." Forecasts:

(Start these teasers 10 days in advance of your opening, building up to the start of your display ad. campaign several days ahead of the playdate. Keep up the idea of the weather forecast and get the most appropriate position obtainable in your newspapers.)

WEATHER—Fair and Funny!
"STEAMBOAT BILL, Jr."

WEATHER—A comedy Cyclone Coming!
"STEAMBOAT BILL, Jr."

WEATHER—A Cloudburst of Laughter!
"STEAMBOAT BILL, Jr."

WEATHER—Sunshine! Nothing Else But!
BUSTER KEATON and
ERNEST TORRENCE in
"STEAMBOAT BILL, Jr."

WEATHER—Always Fair When Good Fellows Get Together!
Next Monday
BUSTER KEATON and
ERNEST TORRENCE in
"STEAMBOAT BILL, Jr."

Accessories Page

Colored Insert Card

Buster Keaton and Ernest Torrence in

"STEAMBOAT BILL, Jr."

Music Scores

Special Orchestra Scores, comprising the authorized themes for "Steamboat Bill, Jr." for both small and large orchestras, may be rented or purchased from

PHOTOPLAY MUSIC CO., Inc.

1520 Broadway, New York, N. Y.

For rental and sale prices for orchestras, or piano and organ, apply direct to Photoplay Music Co., Inc.

Music Cues

Music Cue Sheets on "Steamboat Bill, Jr." may be obtained gratis at all United Artists exchanges.

Cuts and Mats

Apply at your nearest United Artists exchange for cuts and mats on "Steamboat Bill, Jr." See price list attached to this Campaign Book.

Two Trailers

National Screen Service issues a regular Service trailer, 90 feet long, on every United Artists picture. It also issues De Luxe trailers, 200 feet long, on many United Artists pictures.

National Screen Service prices are: $25 per month for a complete service (West of the Rocky Mountains, $30), by which the exhibitor gets a Regluar Service trailer on every picture he plays, regardless of wha company's pictures they are. For $3.50 additional per trailer, the subscriber can obtain a De Luxe trailer on any picture for which one is available.

Non-subscribers to the monthly service pay $5 per Regular Service trailer, with $1.50 remitted when the trailer is returned. They can get De Luxe trailers at $12.50 per trailer, with $5 back when the trailer is returned.

Four months after the release date of a picture a Regular Service trailer is rented at $2.50, with $1 back when it is returned. Address all orders to

NATIONAL SCREEN SERVICE, Inc.

126 W. 46th St., New York, N. Y.

845 S. Wabash Ave., Chicago, Ill.

1922 S. Vermont Ave., Los Angeles, Calif.

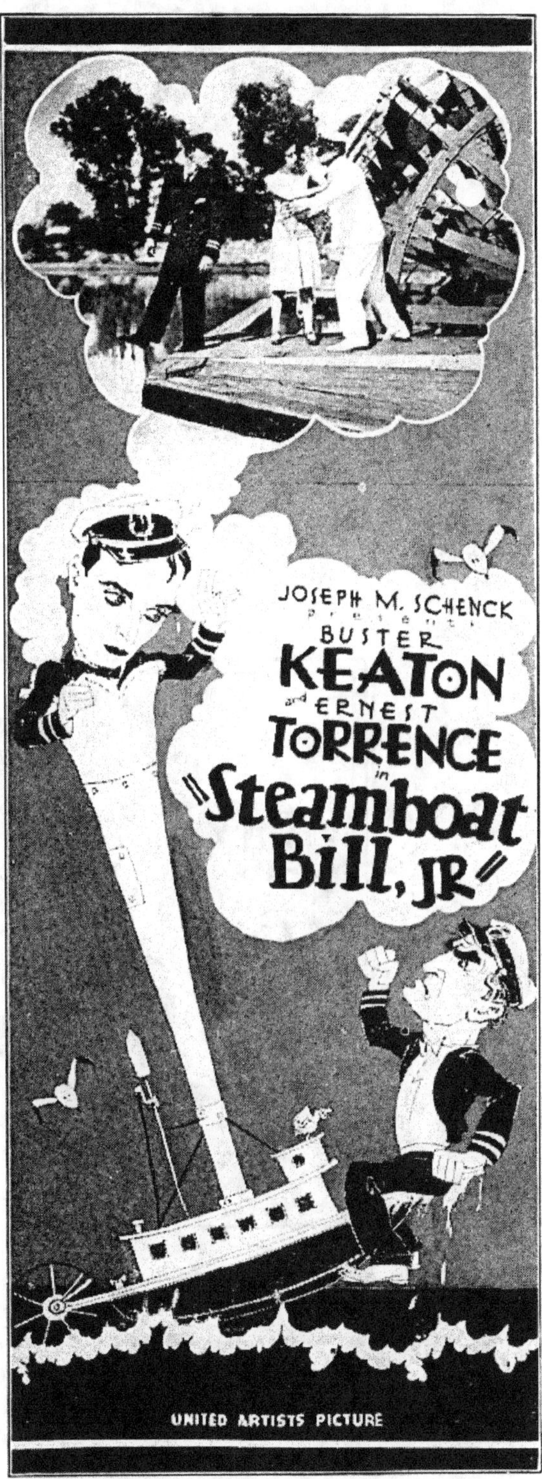

Size—14 in. x 36 in.   Price 25c Each.

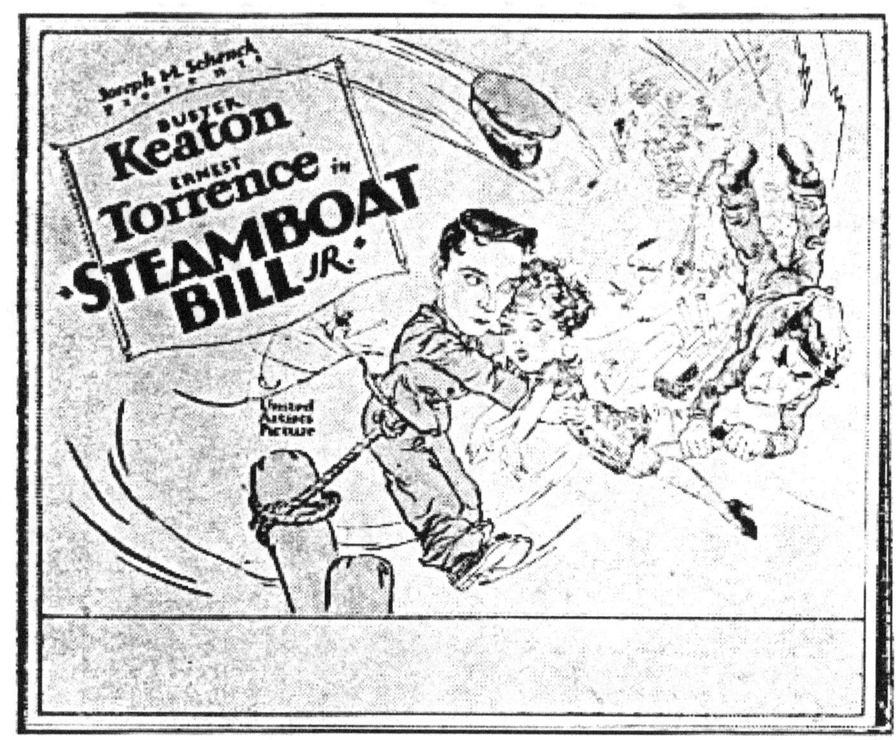

Slide No. 1—Price 15 Cents

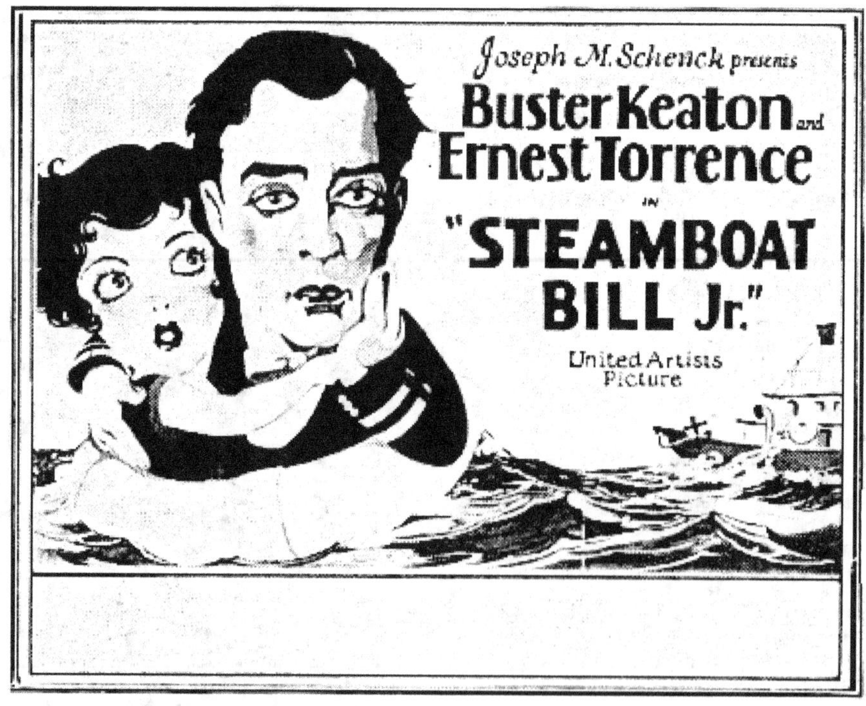

Slide No. 2—Price 15 Cents.

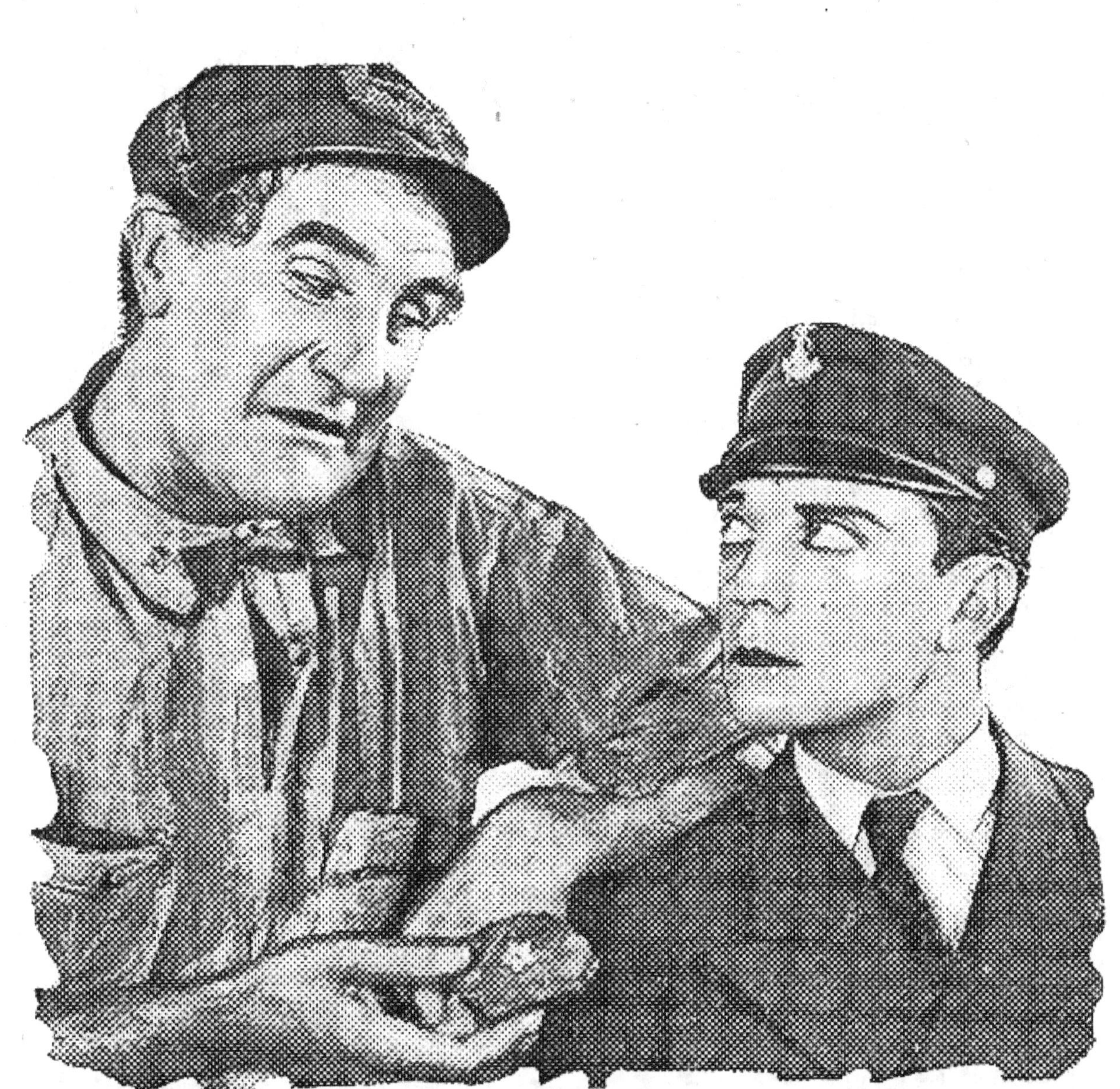

BL-4—Two Col. Scene (Mat 10c; Cut 50c.)

Good Ones Before Opening

BUSTER KEATON HAD TO HAVE A CAT

Many of the greatest motion picture comedy stars and directors, such as Charles Chaplin, Buster Keaton and Charles "Chuck" Reisner, do not work with scripts, or scenarios, when they are making screen features which make the world laugh.

Most of the situations are spontaneous. Some of the hilarious "gags" which occupy only a few minutes on the screen, may have taken days to evolve, while others, which get even bigger laughs, are inspired on the spur of the moment.

During the filming of Buster Keaton's latest United Artists success, "Steamboat Bill Jr.," which is to be shown at the .... next .... the star, his director, Reisner, and Carl Harbaugh, story chief, were discussing the need of something to put over a certain "gag" for the next scene.

Suddenly they decided they needed a cat. But it was during the filming of night scenes, and they were on location, several miles from the nearest town.

"Must have a cat," said Buster.

A half hour later, at 2:30 in the morning, an automobile roared up to the entrance of the Sacramento, California, central police station, a man jumped out and rushed up to the desk sergeant.

The man was out of breath.

"Control yourself!" barked the policeman. "Hurry, tell us what's the trouble. Is it a murder or a robbery?"

"Can I borrow a cat?" gasped Buster's head property man. "My boss is out here twelve miles holding up work on a big picture until we get a cat. Any kind will do. Tom, Angora, alley or otherwise."

"Cat? Are you crazy? Here, Murphy, you better lock this bird up."

But the property man finally convinced the desk sergeant that the request was bona fide, and as the policemen were motion picture fans, they soon rounded up not one cat, but four.

A half hour later a cat had broken into pictures.

See him—or rather, it's a her—in "Steamboat Bill, Jr." and you'll admit the trouble was worth the laugh you enjoy.

RIVER JUNCTION PASSED AWAY LIKE BABYLON

Ever hear of River Junction, California?

You won't find it on the map; in fact, it was in existence only a few months, but during its short life it enjoyed more excitement than some towns do in fifty years.

River Junction was a bustling city constructed especially for a motion picture—"Steamboat Bill Jr.," in which Buster Keaton stars and in which that swashbuckling villain, Ernest Torrence, will be seen at the.................... Theatre.................as a comedian.

The town was erected on the banks of the Sacramento River, across from the historic country where gold was discovered in California. Like some of those early gold rush towns, River Junction served its purpose and then crumbled, though in this case the Keaton company destroyed the community in order to provide thrills and laughs for the public.

Thousands of people—motion picture extras—inhabited the town at the height of its activity. The levee was crowded. Steamboats, barges, launches and other craft dotted the river.

After a few months the Keaton company returned to Hollywood, leaving a ghost town behind.

Even as Babylon and Ninevah, River Junction perished, not because it was wicked, but because the world must be entertained, and in this case the entertainment is a tornado as funny as it is awesome.

"Steamboat Bill Jr.," which was produced by Joseph M. Schenck, president and chairman of the board of directors of United Artists, is the most ambitious picture in Keaton's screen career.

Charles "Chuck" Reisner was behind the megaphone. Devereaux Jennings and Bert Haines, veteran cinematographic aces, headed the camera battery.

The 1927 World's Series games between the New York Yankees and the Pittsburgh Pirates were reported for the The New York Telegram, one of the 26 Scripps-Howard papers, by Buster Keaton, star of "Steamboat Bill, Jr.," at the ....theatre. Buster is a good amateur ball player himself and during the making of "Steamboat Bill, Jr.," along the Sacramento River in California, he and his company played baseball regularly.

A Page of Shorts

Did you know that Ernest Torrence, who plays the chief supporting role opposite Buster Keaton in the United Artists laugh feature, "Steamboat Bill Jr.," which reaches the .... Theatre next .... used to be a musical comedy star? Torrence, an Englishman by birth, is world-famous as a screen villain, but "Steamboat Bill Jr." provides him with a straight comedy role.

———

Another character who has plenty to do, and does it well, is Tom McGuire. He plays Torrence's business rival, the father of the girl.

The direction, by Charles "Chuck" Reisner, shows the expert touch of the man who was Charles Chaplin's right-hand man for several years and who more recently has been directing Syd Chaplin. Reisner can be as proud of "Steamboat Bill Jr." as he was of "Charley's Aunt," "The Better 'Ole" and "The Missing Link," to mention just a few of his previous successes.

All in all, "Steamboat Bill Jr." is an exceptionally good evening's entertainment and a big credit to United Artists, for whom Keaton made this comedy.

———

When Buster Keaton completed several weeks' location scenes in "Steamboat Bill, Jr.", and returned to Hollywood to make the interior scenes in the United Artists comedy special, the technical department discovered that they needed a cross-section of a steamboat pilot house. Wishing to match perfectly the interiors with the exteriors, which were made aboard big river packets on the Sacramento in central California, Keaton has his aides transport bodily one of the pilot houses to the studio in Hollywood. "Steamboat Bill, Jr.", which was directed by Charles "Chuck" Reisner, boasts a cast of notables, including Keaton's co-star, Ernest Torrence, who has temporarily deserted screen villainies for comedy; Marion Byron, petite leading lady, and Tom McGuire, famous character actor.

Buster Keaton's leading lady in the United Artists comedy, "Steamboat Bill Jr.," arriving at the .... Theatre .... is 17-year-old Marion Byron, who was singing and dancing in a Hollywood stage revue when the frozen-faced star discovered her and placed her under contract. Miss Byron, a former Ohio girl, had never been inside a studio until Keaton made her his leading lady. She weighs 100 pounds and is a vivacious brunette. She shares honors in "Steamboat Bill Jr." which was directed by Charles "Chuck" Reisner, with Ernest Torrence, Tom McGuire and other prominent supporting players.

———

Buster Keaton, who is co-starred with Ernest Torrence in "Steamboat Bill, Jr.," soon to come to the.................. theatre, played in nine comedies with Roscoe (Fatty) Arbuckle many years ago.

———

Buster Keaton's real name is Joseph Francis. But this week he is "Steamboat Bill, Jr.," at the.................... theatre.

———

Marion Byron, a new comedienne, is Buster Keaton's leading lady in "Steamboat Bill, Jr.," which also has Ernest Torrence in a co-starring role and which will be seen at the........................ theatre........................... Marion is only seventeen.

———

Who is your favorite comedian? Buster Keaton? Charlie Chaplin? Harold Lloyd? Ray Griffith? Louis Wolheim? Ernest Torrence? Harry Langdon? For the price of one admission you can see two of them, Buster Keaton and Ernest Torrence, in one picture, "Steamboat Bill, Jr.," at the ....theatre....................

———

Harry Houdini, the late wizard of magic, was the man who first called Joseph Francis Keaton, "Buster." Keaton was a babe in arms then. Now he is "Steamboat Bill, Jr.," at the............... theatre. Ernest Torrence is co-starred.

Good Ones Before Opening

ERNEST TORRENCE IS OPPOSITE KEATON

"Playing opposite Buster Keaton, one of the greatest of comedians, was one of the most interesting ventures of my screen career," says Ernest Torrence, who is Buster's father in the United Artists comedy, "Steamboat Bill Jr.," which reaches the .... next ....

"I had long cherished a desire to portray a straight comedy role which would be vastly different from the screen villainies in which I have indulged," he declared. " 'Steamboat Bill Jr.' was a real vacation for me."

Strangely enough, although Torrence was a stage comedian he made his picture debut as a villain in "Tol'able David" with Richard Barthelmess. Among his screen villainies were "Twelve Miles Out" and "Captain Salvation." His achievements in straight character roles include "The King of Kings" and "The Covered Wagon."

LINDBERGH ATE HAM CARVED FROM HIS PIGS

When Buster Keaton was making "Steamboat Bill Jr." his latest United Artists comedy, which reaches the .... next ....
a young man by the name of Charles Lindbergh was making aviation history.

And a farmer in New Jersey was trying to make hay while the sun shone.

"One day, just after Captain Lindbergh had completed his epocal flight to Paris, I received a special delivery, air mail letter," said Buster.

"The writer wanted me to get him a job in pictures because he said he was the fellow who raised the hogs for the ham in the sandwiches which Lindy carried in his plane.

"This chap explained that his home had become a 'shrine', and that people were coming to his place from miles around and whittling away his fences, pig-pens and apple trees for souvenirs. He thought a picture built around his 'shrine' would be timely. He offered to furnish his farm as a location, and suggested that Lindbergh be given the starring role.

"Oh, yes, we wouldn't have to spend any money for a story because his wife had already written a scenario."

NEW KEATON FILM IS COSTLY COMEDY

"Steamboat Bill Jr.," the Buster Keaton comedy for United Artists, which will have its local premiere at the .... Theatre .... is probably the most lavishly produced laugh feature ever made.

From the first glimpse of the frozen-faced star, when he ambles onto the screen as a sappy youth whose own father doesn't even give him credit for being able to do anything but play a ukulele, till the uproarious climax, when Buster turns into the most extraordinary character that ever trod the deck of a stern-wheeler, "Steamboat Bill Jr.", is said to keep audiences in hysterics.

Advance notices call "Steamboat Bill Jr." Keaton at his funniest.

He is the awkward son of a river ship owner, whose position is being threatened by a rival shipper.

The part of Buster's father brings Ernest Torrence as the stumbling, shambling, laughable, but not unlovable old shipowner, out of step with modern business, but stoutly refusing to give up the ship.

Buster's plight throughout the picture is such stuff as laughs are made of. When, for instance, he smuggles into the crude jail where his father is, a huge loaf of bread containing an entire jailbreaking kit, the situation pits the Keaton comedy against the Torrence comedy, contrast making comedy more comical.

Marion Byron, a slender, girlish little newcomer into the United Artists forces, plays the girl opposite Buster's awkward youth. Tom McGuire and Tom Lewis are other prominent members of the cast who share laugh honors.

"Steamboat Bill Jr." was directed by Charles "Chuck" Reisner, former associate of Charles Chaplin and later the megaphone chief for Syd Chaplin during the filming of "The Better 'Ole", "The Missing Link" and other comedies.

Both Keaton and Reisner regard "Steamboat Bill Jr." as the outstanding picture of their careers.

Buster Keaton, whose "Steamboat Bill, Jr.," comes to the........................... theatre .... is teaching his two sons, Joe and Bob, to be "regular fellers." When Buster made "Battling Butler" the children were given a thorough course in boxing; when he made 'The General," they learned Civil War history. But when Buster made "College," the kids continued their elementary studies.

A Page of Shorts

When Buster Keaton and his staff are preparing the story for a feature comedy they believe in getting "far from the maddening crowd," so that's why a party of five men spent a month in the high Sierras during the planning of "Steamboat Bill, Jr.", the frozen-faced star's picture which is at the

....

Buster and his director, Charles "Chuck" Reisner; Harry Brand, general manager of the Keaton studio; Carl Harbaugh, chief of the scenario department; and Sandy Roth, assistant director, left Hollywood without announcing their destination, and nobody but their families knew where they were until they returned.

Some of the funniest situations in "Steamboat Bill, Jr.", were drafted and acted out by Buster and his aides while they were fishing, hunting and hiking in the wildest section of northern California.

California's newest town, which when completed in the record time of three weeks was populated by thousands of people, was built along the shores of the Sacramento river a short distance from the California state capital. The community sprang up especially for Buster Keaton's new United Artists comedy, "Steamboat Bill, Jr.", now at the..............................theatre. Hundred of carpenters and other artisans worked day and night to constuct the mushroom city. The fleets of trucks which plied daily between Sacramento and the made-to-**order town,** carrying quantities of lumber and other materials, were reminiscent of early California days when boom towns sprang into existence overnight.

———

Sandy Roth, who assisted Reisner in the direction of "Steamboat Bill, Jr.", has been "Chuck's" chief aide for years, and he, too, has led an adventurous life, having been a well-known boxer, entertainer and comedy writer before entering the directional ranks.

She is petite Marion Byron, a 17-year-old girl who hadn't even been inside a studio until Keaton selected her as his leading lady.

A score of young actresses, including several who have played leading roles opposite the best known stars, took tests for "Steambot Bill, Jr.", but Miss Byron was the unanimous choice of Buster, Charles "Chuck" Reisner, who directed the comedy, and executives at the Keaton studio. The frozen-faced star was so impressed with the girl's screen possibilities that he has placed her under a five-year contract, the first instance of its kind in the history of the Keaton organization. Miss Byron has been called the greatest find as a comedienne since Mabel Normand first burst into fame.

Because there were no cotton fields along the stretch of river where Buster Keaton and Ernest Torrence made many of the scenes of their United Artists comedy, "Steamboat Bill, Jr.", the frozen-faced star's technical aides grew one overnight. How? Simple. They just got together several cotton plants and transplanted them. In another instance of motion picture resourcefulness, it was found that the river in front of the town that Keaton had constructed for "Steamboat Bill, Jr.", wasn't deep enough to permit large packets to moor at the levee. So the Keaton company negotiated with the captain of a huge dredge, and within twenty-four hours the water was deep enough for a fleet of boats. "Steamboat Bill, Jr.", was directed by Charles "Chuck" Reisner.

———

Buster Keaton's real name is Joseph Francis. But this week he is "Steamboat Bill, Jr.," at the....................theatre.

A Page of Reviews

REVIEW

Buster Keaton, aided and abetted by Ernest Torrence, Director Charles 'Chuck" Reisner, a girl by the name of Marion Byron, and seemingly thousands of other actors and actresses, has made one of the year's funniest pictures.

It is "Steamboat Bill Jr." and it opened at the .... Theatre .... to capacity audiences which all but fell out of their seats at the antics of the frozen-faced star and his assisting mirth-provokers.

The comedy, which was directed by Charles F. Reisner and released by United Artists, is a laugh riot from the opening scene till the cyclonic finish. Cyclonic is right, for the tornado which climaxes "Steamboat Bill Jr." would be, even minus its laughs, a thrill in the most dramatic of dramatic features.

"Steamboat Bill Jr." is different, for it has a real story, with a logical development of plot, has recognized screen favorites in the supporting cast, and doesn't underrate the intelligence of the audience.

The "gags" or comedy situations, are clean, and above all, original.

Buster's characterization of the rah rah boy who comes home from college to help his hardboiled dad (Ernest Torrence) battle a rival steamboat line is the best thing he has ever done. How the rabbit becomes a roaring lion, teaches the rough fellows some new stunts, wins the town magnate's daughter (Marion Byron) and finally rescues the entire population from a tornado and flood, provides Buster with a laugh-a-minute picture which also abounds in love interest and photographic surprises.

"Steamboat Bill Jr." is a story of modern river life, filmed against a beautiful background. The humorous side of steamboating predominates, of course, but there are moments when the thrills overshadow the laughs. Especially is this true too in the final scenes, in which disaster is visited upon the river town and the comedy star turns hero.

Don't miss "Steamboat Bill Jr."— it's 100 per cent entertainment!

Did you know that Ernest Torrence, who plays the chief supporting role opposite Buster Keaton in the United Artists laugh feature, "Steamboat Bill Jr.," which reaches the .... Theatre next .... used to be a musical comedy star? Torrence, an Englishman by birth, is world-famous as a screen villain, but "Steamboat Bill Jr." provides him with a straight comedy role.

REVIEW

Ha! Ha! Ha! Ho! Ho! Ho! ad infinitum.

That's a fair summing up of Buster Keaton's latest laugh riot, "Steamboat Bill, Jr.," which opened............................ at the ....Theatre for ....run.

Easily Keaton's funniest and without a doubt one of the year's biggest pictures, either comedy or dramatic, the feature is, first of all, 100 per cent entertainment.

Originality—a welcome absence of moth-eaten "gags"—marks this modern river comedy all the way through. There is enough slapstick for everybody, but what there is is fresh, clean and not draggy. There is subtle humor —one of the hardest things in the world to put over effectively—and there are a few touches of pathos by way of contrast.

Keaton proves that he is in a class by himself when it comes to motion picture comedy of the type exemplified by "Steamboat Bill Jr." Chaplin and Harold Lloyd have their undisputed niches in the laugh world, and Buster has his. Chaplin's "Circus", Lloyd's "Grandma's Boy" and Keaton's "Steamboat Bill Jr." are perhaps among the funniest pictures ever made.

To the star, of course, go the acting honors, but he does not monopolize the best situations. Chief of the supporting players, and one who proves that he is as great a comedian as he is a villain, is Ernest Torrence. You saw Torrence in "The Covered Wagon," "Tol'able David," "The King of Kings," "Twelve Miles Out," "Captain Salvation" and other dramatic features. Now see him in "Steamboat Bill Jr." and realize the versatility of the man who can play a roaring, brutal rum-runner, a western gun-fighter, a religious disciple or a laugh-provoking steamboat pilot and be convincing in each role.

The comedy starts out with a bang. Keaton, who has been away to a polite boarding school since childhood, returns to a he-man river town just in time to get in on a bitter feud between his dad and a rival steamboat owner. Not having seen his boy for many years, old Bill expects to greet a six-foot plus, two fisted specimen like himself, but instead, a collegiate-garbed, ukulele-toting sap appears on the scene. Then the fun begins!

Bill tries to make a man out of the youth, who promptly complicates matters by falling in love with the daughter of his father's hated rival. Mixup after mixup keeps the audiences in roars until the spectacular ending, when a cyclone, which demolishes a town and jerks large steamboats from their moorings as if they were shells, gives the blundering hero a chance to demonstrate that he's not so dumb after all.

A Page of Shorts

Buster Keaton's last picture was "College." In the beginning of his newest film, "Steamboat Bill, Jr.," at the .... theatre, he returns from college to go to work for his father, Ernest Torrence, on a Mississippi River boat. This is a visual link between the two Keaton pictures.

———

Buster Keaton, whose "Steamboat Bill, Jr.," comes to the............................ theatre ...., has a treasure chest of souvenirs. Among them is an autograph album in which many famous people have inscribed fitting tributes to Buster. Among these is Elsie Janis who, more than ten years ago, wrote:

"There's a dear little man we know
    quite well,
Who around our hearts has cast a spell;
If he made a mistake you never could
    tell,
For he's a mimic, comedian and acro-
    bat as well."

———

Buster Keaton, who is co-starred with Ernest Torrence in "Steamboat Bill, Jr.," soon coming to the.................... theatre, was born in a cyclone and has led a cyclonic existence ever since. As a child he was pummelled around the stage by his father in "The Three Keatons," a vaudeville skit. Buster was in the late World War and was sent home on sick leave. He went to and through "College," and up to the time of going to press his latest casualty was a broken nose, which temporarily suspended production activities.

———

"One Week" Buster Keaton met "Convict Thirteen" who was called "Scarecrow" by "The Neighbors." He said his "Hard Luck" came from "The Haunted House" after "Paleface" had given the "High Sign" to the "Cops" on "The Boat." He was "The Goat" for "His Wife's Relations" at the "Playhouse" but "The Blacksmith" took "Seven Chances" to get him to his "Love Nest" in "The Frozen North." His "Day Dreams" became "Balloonatic" from fear of "Sherlock Holmes, Jr.," and "The Electric House," but "Battling Butler," "The General," "The Navigator" and "The Three Ages" said "Go West," "Our Hospitality" is yours. Go to "College" and see "Steamboat Bill, Jr.," Buster's new picture in which he is co-starred with Ernest Torrence.

Meet "Peanuts." That's the nickname of Marion Byron, leading lady in the Buster Keaton-Ernest Torrence comedy, "Steamboat Bill, Jr." The pintsize comedienne who shares supporting honors in the laugh feature with Tom McGuire and other notables, never had been inside of a studio until Buster Keaton discovered her singing and dancing in a Hollywood stage revue and offered her a five-year contract. When she reported to Director "Chuck" Reisner at the start of work on "Steamboat Bill, Jr.", the members of the company asked what her name was, and she replied: "Peanuts." The name stuck, and that's the way Hollywood discovered the girl who is regarded as the greatest find as a comedienne since Mabel Normand first burst into the limelight.

Hollywood's most surprising screen find plays the feminine lead in the Buster Keaton-Ernest Torrence comedy, "Steamboat Bill, Jr.", which will have its local premiere at the.................. theatre...........................

———

Buster Keaton, whose "Steamboat Bill, Jr." comes to the.......................theatre ...., owns one of the finest autograph albums in existence. One of the first entries in this book was made by the late Lew Dockstader, who foresaw a great future for the miniature frozen-faced star at 'that time, and wrote the following verse:

"Buster, you're a dandy; Buster,
    your're a brick;
Buster, you can make all juveniles look
    sick;
Some day you'll be a great one, the
    captain of the crew,
But don't forget old Wilmington, the
    place of your debut."

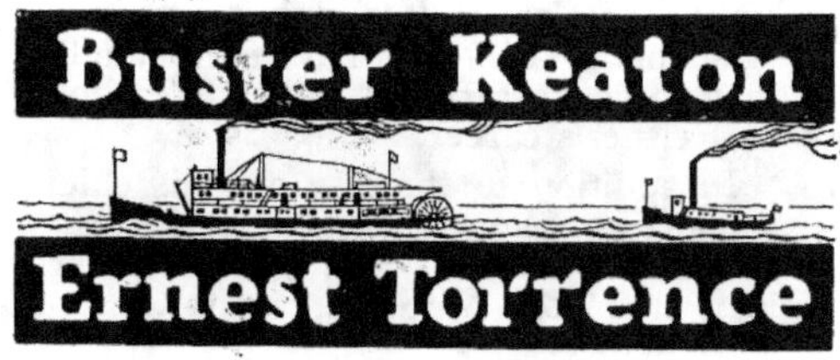

A Page of Reviews

REVIEW

As many laughs as can be crammed into seven thousand feet of film; romance, suspense, thrills—these are some of the elements which go to make up the year's surprise comedy, "Steamboat Bill Jr.," which stars Buster Keaton and presents a number of noted supporting players of the calibre of Ernest Torrence.

Keaton's new United Artists laugh feature is convulsing capacity audiences at the .... Theatre, and this writer takes pride in especially recommending "Steamboat Bill Jr." as one of the season's "guaranteed pictures."

The fast-moving story of river life is Keaton at his funniest and Torrence in his most interesting role. Photoplaygoers who invariably associate the noted character actor with villainous parts are due for a shock when they see him sharing laughs in his portrayal of Buster's hardboiled, swashbuckling dad, a modern river pilot with a hatred for mollycoddles, and with a penchant for getting into trouble.

How his son, "Steamboat Bill Jr.," as played by Keaton, turns from sap to hero, wins the town belle, defeats a gang of river rowdies intent upon ruining him, and finally rescues the entire community from a tornado and flood, forms a background for scores of mirthful situations.

The settings in the big comedy are as spectacular as the action itself.

A typical lower Mississippi river town suddenly given a new lease on life by a bitter war between rival steamboat owners! Thousands of townspeople taking sides in the feud! Buildings swept into the river by a cyclone! Large packets helpless in the storm! And a laugh a minute throughout the excitement, which starts with the first scene and reaches its climax in the wildest, funniest ending ever shown on the screen.

The director of "Steamboat Bill Jr." was Charles "Chuck" Reisner, former right-hand man of Charles Chaplin and the megaphone expert responsible for Syd Chaplin's "Charley's Aunt", "The Better 'Ole" and "The Missing Link." In the opinion of last night's audience "Steamboat Bill Jr." has more laughs than any feature in either Keaton's or Reisner's career.

In addition to the star and his chief supporting player, Torrence, the cast includes Marion Byron, petite leading lady and Tom McGuire, veteran character actor.

REVIEW

To the accompaniment of river shipping wars, tornados and love affairs, Buster Keaton is leading a laugh carnival this week at the .... Theatre, where the frozen-faced star's new United Artists comedy, "Steamboat Bill Jr.", is showing in this territory for the first time.

Keaton has made several highly successful feature comedies during his career—"Seven Chances," "The Navigator," "Battling Butler," and "College", to mention a few—but "Steamboat Bill Jr." has them all beat for abundance of laughs, originality of story, colorful background and excellent supporting cast.

The star, still his frozen-faced self, is a master of subtle comedy and pantomine in "Steamboat Bill Jr." as well as the limb-risking, blundering farceur whom the lovers of broader risibilities prefer. He also gives the other members of the company opportunity to glean their share of the laughs, especially Ernest Torrence, who is as funny in Buster's picture as he has been villainous in most of his previous vehicles. Torrence's venture into straight comedy stamps him as a gloom chaser of the first degree.

Another supporting player who should be heard from as a result of "Steamboat Bill Jr." is Marion Byron, a little comedienne who has a rollicking love affair with the star. This hoyden has a distinctive naivete greatly reminiscent of Mabel Normand. Tom McGuire, the veteran character actor, is another sharer of honors in Keaton's river comedy.

"Steamboat Bill Jr." is replete with thrilling situations. Steamboat crashes, fights and a cyclone which demolishes an entire town and makes a hero out of the blundering character played by Keaton are included in the entertainment menu.

One of the biggest laughs of the picture is the scene in which Keaton, by a ruse, liberates his father (Torrence) from the town bastile.

The brilliant direction is the work of Charles "Chuck" Reisner, former right-hand man of Charles Chaplin and more recently the director of Syd Chaplin's comedies.

The titles in "Steamboat Bill Jr." are a scream.

A Page of Shorts

Competition may be the life of trade but it's the death of a Mississippi River boat in "Steamboat Bill, Jr.," the new United Artists comedy at the...................... theatre, in which Buster Keaton and Ernest Torrence are co-starred. The old order and the new modernistic go-getter are strongly contrasted in two river boats which are democratized by a cyclone wholly lacking in discrimination.

———

Buster Keaton, whose "Steamboat Bill, Jr.," comes to the............................ theatre .... is teaching his two sons, Joe and Bob, to be "regular fellers." When Buster made "Battling Butler" the children were given a thorough course in boxing; when he made 'The General," they learned Civil War history. But when Buster made "College," the kids continued their elementary studies.

———

What are the first names of Buster Keaton, Babe Ruth, Jack Dempsey, and Gene Tunney? Eugene is not Tunney's first name; it is James. Dempsey is really William Harrison Dempsey and Ruth is George Herman Ruth. Keaton is Joseph Francis Keaton and he is at the................................theatre now in "Steamboat Bill, Jr." Ernest Torrence is also starred in the picture of Mississippi River boats and cyclones.

———

Ernest Torrence, who is co-starred with Buster Keaton in "Steamboat Bill, Jr.," at the.................................theatre, is as Scotch as Sir Harry Lauder. And as big-hearted as Santa Claus. Ernest is doing comedy as a relief from his heavy dramatic work in "The King of Kings," "The Covered Wagon" and other films.

———

Buster Keaton gradually is covering the United States with locales of his pictures. "College" was laid in the golden west, "where land and water meet"—California. "The General" was inspired by an incident of the American Civil War, during which an engine chased another puffing locomotive through Georgia. Now, in "Steamboat Bill, Jr.," Keaton and Ernest Torrence are seen on the deck of an old Mississippi River boat. The new comedy comes to the..................................... theatre...................................

Moving locales for moving pictures seems to be a new wrinkle put over by Buster Keaton. In "The General," his first United Artists picture, a Civil War locomotive was the scene of most of the action, with Buster clambering up and down smokestacks. Now, in "Steamboat Bill, Jr.," at the...................... theatre, the action takes place on a Mississippi River steamboat. If Buster sticks to means of transportation, he'll have to make an airplane comedy soon.

———

A cyclone is the kick finish to Buster Keaton and Ernest Torrence's co-starring comedy, "Steamboat Bill, Jr.," at the .... theatre. The tornado sweeps through the Mississippi River country where "Steamboat Bill" is having a hard time with his side-wheeler, the "Stonewall Jackson," because of heavy competition from his rich rival, the important Mr. King. More than a quarter of a million dollars' destruction is wrought in behalf of laughter. The funny part of it is that the town of Pickway, Kansas, and the birthplace of Buster, not so far from the scene of the Keaton film was blown off the map by a tornado shortly after Keaton was born there in the rectory of a church in which his parents took refuge from the storm.

———

Natalie Talmadge Keaton, wife of Buster Keaton, who will soon be seen in "Steamboat Bill, Jr.," gave up a promising career as a screen actress to make a home for her actor-husband.

———

A bit of pantomime which Buster Keaton employs in "Steamboat Bill, Jr." is said by manager.......................of the.......................theatre to rank with the memorable Oceana Roll danced by Charlie Chaplin's biscuits in "The Gold Rush." Keaton's film father, Ernest Torrence, is in jail and mad at the son whose stupidity put him there. The penitent youth arrives at the jail with a loaf of bread for his father, but the father refuses it. Then Keaton pantomimes to the tune of "The Prisoner's Song" the fact that he has the means of escape with him. Manager................. of the .... says it's a howl.

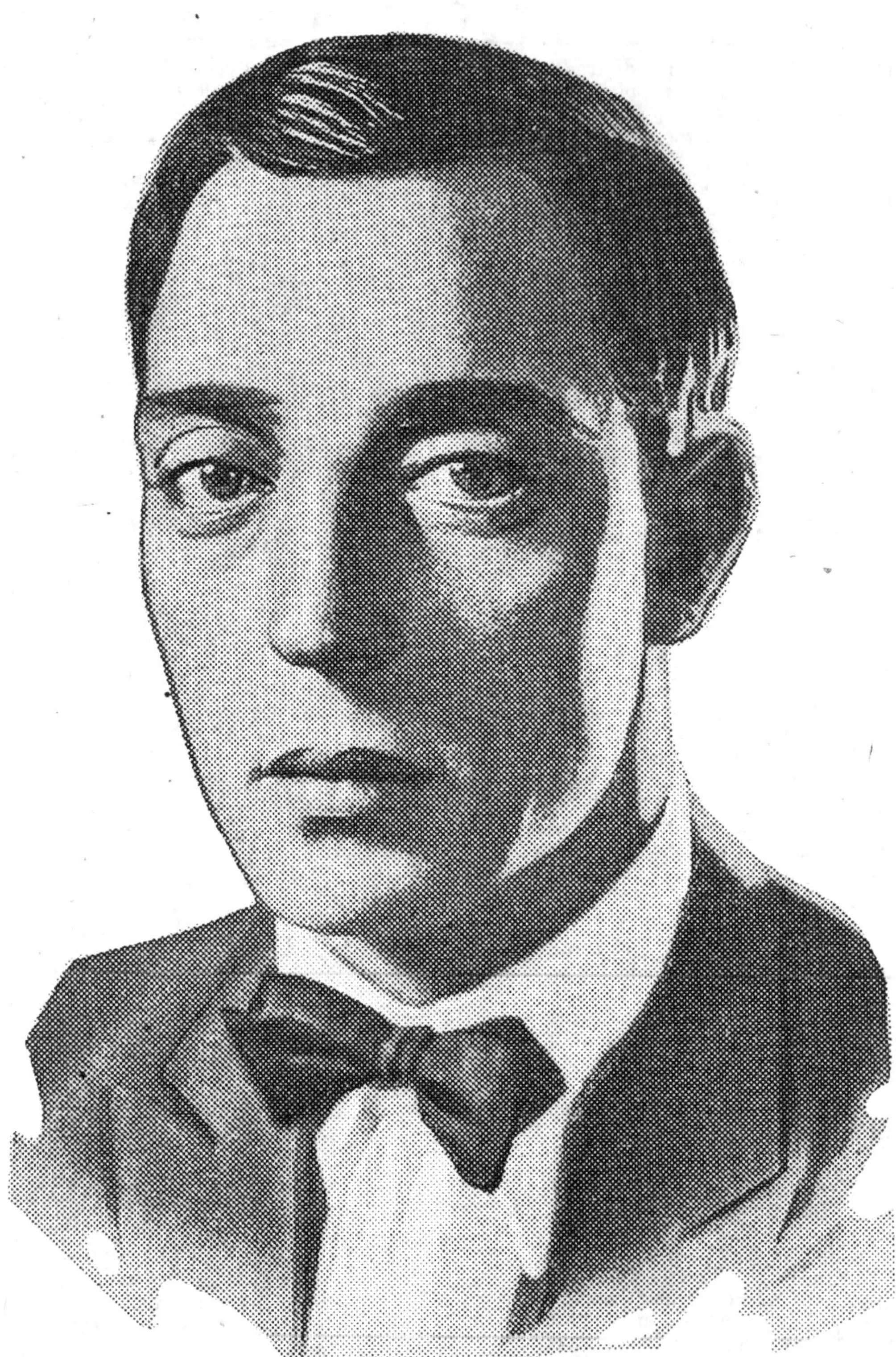

BUSTER KEATON

BK-2—Two Col. Scene (Mat 10c; Cut 50c)

News of the Personalities

WHAT BEING WIFE OF FILM STAR MEANS

(By Natalie Talmadge Keaton, wife of Buster Keaton, in "Steamboat Bill, Jr.," at the ....)

It means seeing your husband come home almost every night as someone else—a sailor or a college boy, or possibly a railroad engineer, followed by cameramen and hearing them talk way into the night about the seriousness of being funny.

It means having dinner one night at nine and the next night at six.

It also means running one's house as a home should be run—for the individuals rather than for the furniture.

It means—well—above everything leading an interesting if somewhat diversified life.

Discounting the fact that the salary of a motion picture star is usually sufficient to cover the necessities and many of the luxuries of life, there are still many good reasons why it is nice to be married to a successful screen star.

The everyday things of life seem to interest us more intensely. Like all people in the picture world, we take nothing casually. To us, almost unconsciously, every situation is dramatic and our effort is to bring something to life rather than to get something from it.

That I suppose is the real reason—we have made the world romantic by thinking it so—and a husband who spends his life trying to make the world laugh is bound to be amusing to his wife.

In Hollywood a film star is an actor or actress whose name is mentioned before that of the picture. A star appears "in" a picture. A featured player is one whose name follows that of the picture, the film being "with" so and so. In "Steamboat Bill, Jr.," the United Artists comedy which comes to the .... theatre........................

Which of Buster Keaton's pictures did you like best? The last "College," or "The General," or "The Navigator?" His newest, in which Ernest Torrence also appears, is "Steamboat Bill, Jr.," and it comes to the.................................. theatre...............................

"LUCKY BREAKS"

By Buster Keaton

(Star of "Steamboat Bill Jr." which reaches the...................... next.......................)

Life for me has just been one lucky break after another.

I arrived upon this planet during a storm in a little Kansas town—a storm blew down the tent where my mother and father were working a medicine show with the late Harry Houdini. The stork had already sent word he was on his way, so mother wanted to give him a proper reception and started, with my father, for the nearest parish-house. They got into the church by mistake, so that was where the stork delivered me—making him a sort of bird-of-pray.

But that was a lucky break, wasn't it, coming into the world under such proper conditions?

As for my lucky break in pictures, that was my decision to take forty dollars a week to make two-reel comedies for Joseph M. Schenck instead of accepting several hundred for an act at the New York Winter Garden.

From the time of my entrance into this vale of tears, I had appeared in an act with my parents, travelling over the world in so doing. When I was twenty-one the Shuberts asked me to go into musical comedy at the Winter Garden.

This was a very good offer and I was rehearsing when Joe Schenck called to ask me if I'd like to make a series of two-reel pictures for him at $40 weekly.

All my life I had travelled and the idea of settling down in one spot was more attractive to me than the actual money gain. Besides, I liked Mr. Schenck and felt he knew what he was talking about when he assured me there was a future for me in motion pictures.

And so I took the forty dollars, and consider that decision the luckiest break of all my lucky breaks.

Natalie Talmadge Keaton, wife of Buster Keaton, who will soon be seen in "Steamboat Bill, Jr.," gave up a promising career as a screen actress to make a home for her actor-husband.

News of the Personalities

Who is your favorite comedian? Buster Keaton? Charlie Chaplin? Harold Lloyd? Ray Griffith? Louis Wolheim? Ernest Torrence? Harry Langdon? For the price of one admission you can see two of them, Buster Keaton and Ernest Torrence, in one picture, "Steamboat Bill, Jr.," at the ....theatre....................

———

Harry Houdini, the late wizard of magic, was the man who first called Joseph Francis Keaton, "Buster." Keaton was a babe in arms then. Now he is "Steamboat Bill, Jr.," at the................ theatre. Ernest Torrence is co-starred.

———

Did you know that Ernest Torrence, who plays the chief supporting role opposite Buster Keaton in the United Artists laugh feature, "Steamboat Bill Jr.," which reaches the .... Theatre next .... used to be a musical comedy star? Torrence, an Englishman by birth, is world-famous as a screen villain, but "Steamboat Bill Jr." provides him with a straight comedy role.

———

Another character who has plenty to do, and does it well, is Tom McGuire. He plays Torrence's business rival, the father of the girl.

The direction, by Charles "Chuck" Reisner, shows the expert touch of the man who was Charles Chaplin's right-hand man for several years and who more recently has been directing Syd Chaplin. Reisner can be as proud of "Steamboat Bill Jr." as he was of "Charley's Aunt," "The Better 'Ole" and "The Missing Link," to mention just a few of his previous successes.

All in all, "Steamboat Bill Jr." is an exceptionally good evening's entertainment and a big credit to United Artists, for whom Keaton made this comedy.

Marion Byron, a new comedienne, is Buster Keaton's leading lady in "Steamboat Bill, Jr.," which also has Ernest Torrence in a co-starring role and which will be seen at the........................ theatre........................... Marion is only seventeen.

———

Who is your favorite comedian? Buster Keaton? Charlie Chaplin? Harold Lloyd? Ray Griffith? Louis Wolheim? Ernest Torrence? Harry Langdon? For the price of one admission you can see two of them, Buster Keaton and Ernest Torrence, in one picture, "Steamboat Bill, Jr.," at the ....theatre....................

———

Buster Keaton's leading lady in the United Artists comedy, "Steamboat Bill Jr.," arriving at the .... Theatre .... is 17-year-old Marion Byron, who was singing and dancing in a Hollywood stage revue when the frozen-faced star discovered her and placed her under contract. Miss Byron, a former Ohio girl, had never been inside a studio until Keaton made her his leading lady. She weighs 100 pounds and is a vivacious brunette. She shares honors in "Steamboat Bill Jr." which was directed by Charles "Chuck" Reisner, with Ernest Torrence, Tom McGuire and other prominent supporting players.

———

Buster Keaton, who is co-starred with Ernest Torrence in "Steamboat Bill, Jr.," soon to come to the.................. theatre, played in nine comedies with Roscoe (Fatty) Arbuckle many years ago.

———

Buster Keaton's real name is Joseph Francis. But this week he is "Steamboat Bill, Jr.," at the.................... theatre.

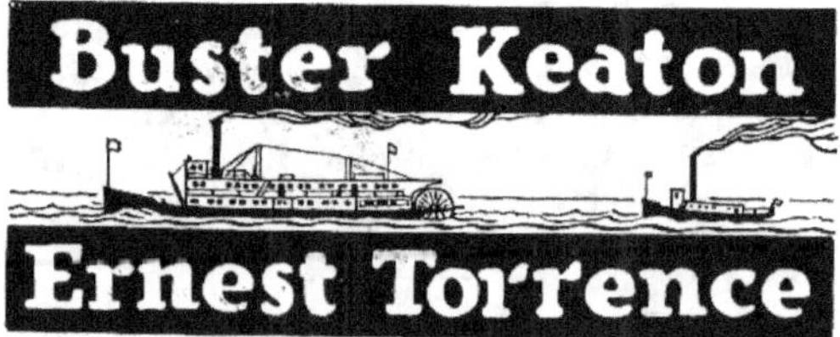

Advance Or During Run

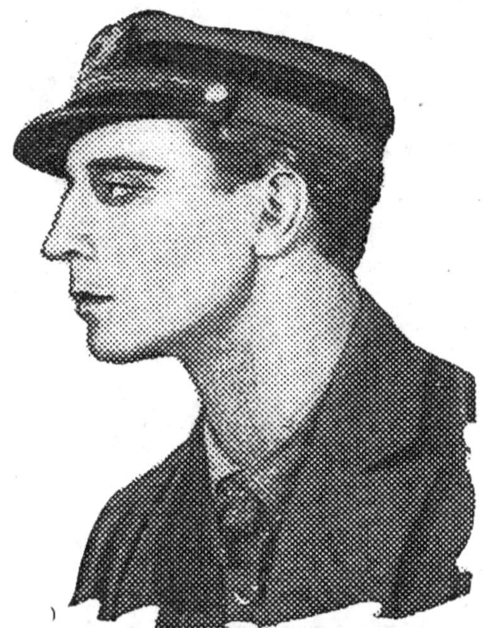

BL-1—One Col. Scene

BUSTER KEATON WAS ANXIOUS TO FIGHT

Did you know that one of Buster's boyhood ambitions was to be a professional prize-fighter? While touring the world as a member of his parents' vaudeville act, "The Three Keatons," Buster met all the great and near great in fistiana. John L. Sullivan, James J. Corbett, Tom Sharkey, James J. Jeffries and other stars of the prize ring patted little Buster on the head and predicted he would be famous some day. The youth outgrew his professional pugilistic ambitions, and became instead an amateur boxer of note. He is still an enthusiast and numbers among his thousands of friends practically all the ring champions of today. When he is not making a picture he rarely misses a championship bout. Buster's latest picture, "Steamboat Bill Jr.," which arrives at the .... Theatre next .... shows his proficiency with his fists.

MY IDEA OF HAPPINESS

By Buster Keaton

(Star of "Steamboat Bill Jr.," which reaches the____________ next_____________________)

Distant fields are always supposed to be the greenest, and the world in general is usually credited with wishing for something it hasn't got, but in my own case, I am happier now than I would be under any other circumstances or in any other clime.

It has taken me years, however, to make my idea of happiness come true, and there were many, many times that I thought I would never reach my goal. For from the day of my birth and up until about a decade ago, I feared I never would have a home.

The reason was because I never stayed in one place long enough to call it home. My parents were show people; I was a member of their act practically since babyhood, and we roamed the world.

I wonder if the average person, born and reared in a real home atmosphere, realizes how much traveling show people secretly yearn for a chance to settle down? Jumping from city to city, country to country,—that sounds exciting and adventurous. It is—for a while, but just spend the first twenty years of your life doing it, and see how glad you'll be to acquire a permanent postoffice address.

To have a home and a family was always my ambition, and I realized the first part of it when I quit vaudeville and entered motion pictures. A few years later I met THE girl. My wife thought enough of a home to abandon a very promising career in pictures. Perhaps you've heard of Natalie Talmadge.

Now there are two little Keatons, and of course, like all mothers and fathers, we think they're the finest boys in the world.

And that's my idea of happiness.

"We found married life the best fun possible. We don't go about much; we are great 'homebodies'. Buster rides, rows, swims, golfs, plays tennis, baseball, handball and football. I like swimming and golf.

Advance Or During Run

MRS. BUSTER KEATON IS HAPPILY WED

Buster Keaton's wife, Natalie Talmadge Keaton, always accompanies her famous husband when he goes on location with his company, and during the filming of the comedian's United Artists feature, "Steamboat Bill Jr.," which reaches the ·..............Theatre next .... while they were at Sacramento, Calif., making steamboating scenes, someone asked Mrs. Keaton for her happy matrimonial recipe.

"Because we are two romantics; we like the same things, laugh at the same jokes, love family life, and have in common our sons, Joe and Bob," replied Mrs. Keaton, who gave up a screen career to star domestically. She is content to let Norma and Constance uphold the honor of the Talmadge family on the screen.

Natalie Keaton tells how Norma used to take her to the old Vitagraph studio in Brooklyn and permit her to sit on the sidelines and watch the stars of that period. She confesses that she "fell in love" several times, but that the actors she adored didn't know anything about it.

"I had a schoolgirl 'crush' on Tony Moreno, and then I thought that Francis Bushman was my ideal; and then I scrapped both of them for dashing Maurice Costello—'Dimples,' everybody called him in those days," laughed Natalie, as Buster, sitting beside her on the set, exclaimed, "Ah, ha, now it's all coming out!"

"Yes," she continued, "those were the heroes of my kid days. The comedian of those days—it was two or three years before the war—were not as subtle as Buster. They went in for slapstick, not character touches. John Bunny was in his heyday. He was getting, I think, $200 a week. That made him look like an emperor to us.

"Regarding Buster. Well, the late Harry Houdini owned a tent show in partnership with Joe and Myra Keaton. A cyclone blew down the tent, and Buster arrived in the world that night.

"He had a pretty rough passage as a youngster. He started his stage career as a tot, and later was what one might call the 'juvenile lead' in a vaudeville act, 'The Three Keatons'. Then the new industry of the movies caught him up; but he wasn't exactly world-famous or wealthy when the war came, and Buster went overseas as a private in the American Army.

"Then he came into the pictures again, and achieved stardom. Also, we met.

"I was working as assistant to the studio manager when our romance started. We sort of thought we liked one another. Buster was shy. He blushed when he first asked me out to dinner. But, having asked me once, he asked me a lot more times, in quick succession—in case, he told me afterwards when we knew one another better, he got out of practice and lost his nerve.

"When I left Hollywood to join Constance in the East, Buster got agitated. A steady stream of letters and telegrams came. And then, came Buster himself. It was a forlorn Buster, walking with the aid of crutches—he had been injured in a film.

"Obviously, he had to be comforted. Obviously, also, we couldn't separate again. In fact, we decided then and there that we couldn't separate again for all the rest of our lives; and in the spring of 1921 we were married at Norma's country home.

WINDSTORM FILMED IN KEATON COMEDY

When a terrific wind storm leveled a populous town on the banks of the Sacramento River, across from the California state capital, and uprooted trees, blew steamboats and other craft from their moorings, everybody was happy.

It was all part of a motion picture comedy, "Steamboat Bill Jr.," in which Buster Keaton and Ernest Torrence star under the Joseph M. Schenck banner for United Artists.

The town required several weeks to build, and up until the day of the storm the thriving community enjoyed a peaceful existence. When the hurricane had subsided all that was left of the several acres of buildings was debris.

The storm lasted all day. Scores of wind machines and steel cables attached to tractors out of camera range were the chief instruments of destruction. Buildings toppled into the river as if struck by a giant unseen hand. Clouds of dust were visible for miles around. Thousands of people journeyed to the scene of the excitement to witness the synthetic holocaust.

Keaton's made-to-order town in "Steamboat Bill Jr." which comes to the .... next .... was the most expensive set ever constructed for a comedy and thrill on the screen was so complete that there was nothing left to salvage.

Supporting Keaton in the cast are Ernest Torrence, the famous portrayer of villainous roles who is playing his first comedy role; Marion Byron, 17-year-old leading lady; Tom McGuire and Tom Lewis.

Advance Or During Run

BERNHARDT TAUGHT BUSTER KEATON

"Steamboat Bill, Jr.," the Buster Keaton comedy for United Artists which will have its premiere at the .... Theatre ...., is undoubtedly Buster's funniest comedy.

Keaton, like most humorists, has a serious side. He is, for instance, quite serious about the bringing-up of his two children. In writing about it, he said:

"The theatre educated me. By meeting great people like Bernhardt, by hearing her recite beautiful bits of poetry. Because I was a child and because she loved children, she would explain to me in simple words the meaning of the story. I studied geography by traveling all over the world. At about twelve years of age, I could draw a map and put almost everything in it that should be put in it. A child of the theatre is really to be envied because he learns by playing.

"I decided that when my two youngsters should reach the age of reason, which is four years old, in my estimation, that they, too, would learn, as I had learned, constantly and through pleasure as well as through the usual kindergarten experiences. In 'Battling Butler,' I had a boxing expert come to our house for three months to teach me how to box. At the end of three months, both of those boys of mine had some scientific knowledge of boxing. You couldn't have paid them to leave me while I was taking a lesson.

"When we made 'The General,' which by the way is the name of the engine, they became so steeped in Civil War history that they were fighting over the different uniforms worn by the members of the cast. They hung around that engine that we had made, which is an exact reproduction of the original of 'The General' now on view in the North Carolina and St. Louis Railroad station in Nashville, Tenn., until they knew every screw and wheel in it. From this picture, in fact from every picture that they have watched in the making, they have learned the power of details. They know the labor that it takes before pleasure is achieved."

BUSTER AND ERNEST BOTH GOT ALL WET

Buster Keaton and Ernest Torrence changed their daily dozen to their daily ducking during the filming of "Steamboat Bill Jr.," the spectacular United Artists comedy of a thousand laughs which comes to the .... Theatre ....

The frozen-faced star and his co-starring player in the Joseph M. Schenck production like to swim, but they received an overdose of bathing with all their clothes on.

When the Keaton company spent two months on location along the Sacramento River in central California, Buster and Torrence, who has temporarily deserted screen villainies for straight comedy, fell off of steamboats and decks to provide laughs in the feature directed by Charles "Chuck" Reisner, and when they returned to the studio in Hollywood for the final scenes, a huge tank was constructed so they could continue the immersions.

Both actors were forced to change their clothes as many as five times a day.

"Steamboat Bill Jr." is described as a modern story of river life which is as thrilling as it is laughable. Torrence, playing a hardboiled steamboat captain, tries to make a real man out of a sap son, with surprising results.

Among the members of the cast are Marion Byron, 17-year-old unknown chosen by Buster as his leading lady; Tom Lewis, who formerly appeared in the Ziegfeld Follies, and Tom McGuire, veteran character actor.

During the filming of the river scenes Buster used as many as two hundred extras at one time.

Keaton has made three United Artists pictures without a rest, and, with the completion of "Steamboat Bill Jr." the star started on his first real vacation in years.

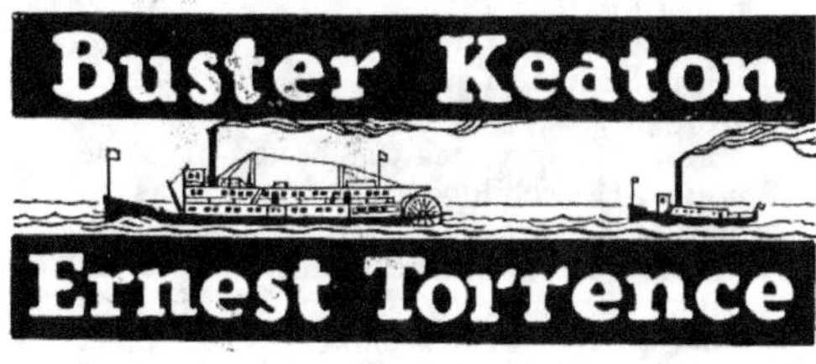

Advance Or During Run

BORN "JOE" BUT WAS RE-NAMED "BUSTER"

What's in a name?

Lots, thinks Buster Keaton, whose latest United Artists comedy "Steamboat Bill Jr.," which was filmed under the Joseph M. Schenck banner and directed by Charles "Chuck" Reisner, reaches the ....Theatre next ....

"If my parents had christened me Algernon, or Geoffrey or something like that, I don't know what would have happened. As a matter of fact, I was named Joseph, after my father, whose father bore the same name. But I became Buster at the age of six months, and I believe my name has helped in bringing what screen success has come my way."

Buster and his wife, Natalie Talmadge Keaton, a sister of Norma and Constance, have two sons. When the boys were born they were named Joe and Bob, not Joseph and Robert, but just plain Joe and Bob, and the Keatons believe they have given their boys a good naming start in life.

FLEET OF BOATS USED FOR NEW KEATON FILM

A fleet of large steamers, barges, launches and dredges were leased or built for Buster Keaton's new United Artists picture, "Steamboat Bill Jr.," a spectacular comedy of modern river life, which is to be shown at the ....Theatre next............ A town, populated by several thousand people, was built on the banks of the Sacramento River, across from the California state capital, and then destroyed in a synthetic cyclone to provide thrills and laughs. Ernest Torrence, noted character actor; Marion Byron and Tom McGuire are among the supporting players in "Steamboat Bill Jr." Charles "Chuck" Reisner, whose directorial career includes features for Charles Chaplin and Syd Chaplin, was the man behind the megaphone during the filming of Keaton's biggest production to date.

Buster Keaton, who is co-starred with Ernest Torrence in "Steamboat Bill, Jr.," now at the............................... Theatre, is an amateur boxer of some note. His childhood ambition was to become a famous boxer, and although he outgrew these dreams of the boxing ring, he numbers among his friends some of the greatest boxers of all time. Charles "Chuck" Reisner, director of "Steamboat Bill, Jr." was also a prizefighter. He was so proficient as a songwriter, boxer, actor, director and "gag" man, that he had some difficulty in deciding which vocation he would follow.

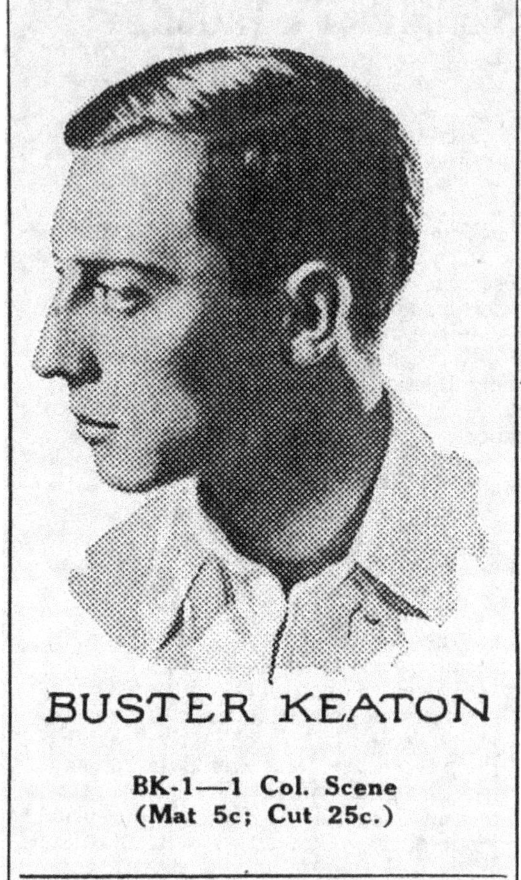

BK-1—1 Col. Scene
(Mat 5c; Cut 25c.)

Buster Keaton is Steamboat Bill, Jr. in his latest comedy, which will head the bill at ....

For this picture, Buster put his "iron face" into training for a month. Exactly four weeks before he went on the set as Steamboat Bill, Jr., Keaton gave up smiling—for he does smile in private life—often a wide, generous grin that changes the entire expression of his face.

Keaton generally takes three weeks before shooting starts on a picture to train his face by keeping it absolutely expressionless. The extra week for Steamboat Bill, Jr. may have been because of Ernest Torrence, who was co-starred with him. Torrence loves to "break up" anyone who acts with him. To "break up" in picture parlance is to make people laugh when they don't want to.

However, Buster came before the camera with his frozen expression and not once during the picture was Torrence able to "break him up." The frozen face never melted.

More Advance News

KEATON DRESSES IN ROOMS WITH NAMES

Buster Keaton had to add another dressing room to his studio when he completed his new United Artists comedy, "Steamboat Bill Jr.," which was produced by Joseph M. Schenck and directed by Charles "Chuck" Reisner.

The studio didn't particularly need another dressing room, for there were dozens already, but Buster insisted on following a precedent which he established when he started in motion pictures more than ten years ago.

The frozen-faced comedian began naming dressing rooms after his pictures. He has always named them after his previous pictures, and as the supply of rooms was exhausted after the completion of "Steamboat Bill Jr.," the carpenters got busy and made a small addition to the film plant.

When actors sign to play in a Keaton picture they are assigned to dressing rooms by name, not number. They are told to dress in "The General," "College," "Battling Butler," "Go West," "Seven Chances," "Navigation," or in one of the many others, including "The Blacksmith," "Convict 13," "The Scarecrow," "The Haunted House," "Neighbors," "The High Sign," "Hard Luck," "The Playhouse," "The Goat," "The Paleface," "The Boat," "Hospitality," etc.

"So long as I keep making pictures at my own studio there will be no shortage of dressing rooms," opined Keaton.

"Steamboat Bill Jr" will be shown at the.................... Theatre next .... Ernest Torrence heads Keaton's supporting cast.

Two of the members of the cast of Buster Keaton's "Steamboat Bill, Jr.," at the .... Theatre ...., were on the legitimate stage before joining the movie ranks. Marion Byron had a small part in a Los Angeles musical comedy; Ernest Torrence had several musical comedy leads before the movies won him over.

BARRYMORE CALLS KEATON FINE ACTOR

John Barrymore in a recent article said in reference to Buster Keaton, "One of the finest motion picture actors that I can think of is Buster Keaton, who has the necessary and instinctive genius for his craft. And one of the elements of his great success lies in his having acquired the facial impassivity of a blackboard in a grammar school, on which he slenderly traces patterns that photograph like Maryon's etchings. And that is pretty fine stuff in black and white."

So much for the legend that actors are jealous. As a matter of fact, their appreciation of each other's work is most generous and intelligent.

In Hollywood, while a picture is being made, they visit each other on the set, are sympathetic in their attitude and in no way display the enviousness credited to them.

It is of course true that the motion picture actor today differs from the actor of other days. He is a householder, seldom travels except to go on location; the business side of his art is more systematized and, provided he is a star, he has his special type of role.

While the emotion of jealousy still exists, it does not dominate the moving picture element of Hollywood.

Throughout his latest picture, "Steamboat Bill, Jr.," in which Buster Keaton is co-starred with Ernest Torrence, there was not the slightest fight for the center of the set.

Ernest Torrence, who will be seen in "Steamboat Bill, Jr." at the............... Theatre ...., was discovered by Henry King about eight years ago, while Torrence was playing in "The Night Boat," a musical comedy. Thereafter, Mr. Torrence has appeared exclusively in motion pictures.

Ernest Torrence, who is co-starred with Buster Keaton in "Steamboat Bill, Jr.," is a musical comedy star of considerable fame. He appeared in musical comedies in Great Britain for fifteen years before coming to America.

More Advance News

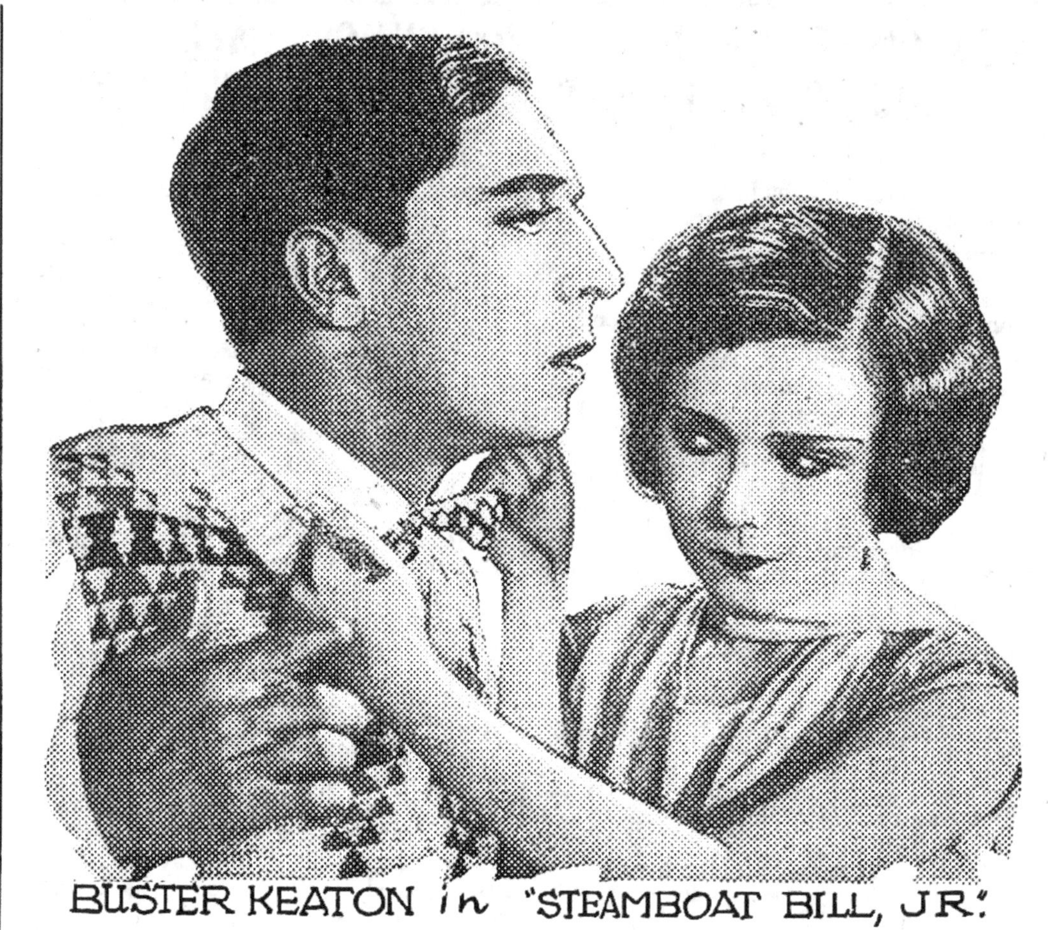

BL-3—Two Col. Scene (Mat 10c; Cut 50c.)

FACTS ABOUT "BILL"

1. Buster Keaton and Ernest Torrence,—two of filmdom's biggest stars,—in the same picture, "Steamboat Bill, Jr." "Little Bill" and "Big Bill" are a comination as invincible in films as Bill Tilden and Bill Johnston in tennis.

2. Charles F. "Chuck" Reisner, director, made Syd Chaplin's "The Better 'Ole." He was also Charlie Chaplin's right hand man in making of "The Gold Rush."

3. Marion Byron, a 17-year-old "find," is Keaton's leading lady. Tom Lewis and Tom McGuire are other notables in the cast.

4. The story by Carl Harbaugh is that of a famous old Mississippi River steamboat and its modern rival,—with all the thrills and humor connoted by such boats in contest on the muddy waters.

5. "Steamboat Bill, Jr.", is physically the biggest comedy in which either Buster Keaton or Ernest Torrence has appeared. It cost more than half a million dollars to produce.

6. The climax of this picture is a tornado. The destruction wrought in the cause of laughter amounted to $255,000.

General Advance Stories

"STEAMBOAT BILL, JR.," BRINGS BUSTER KEATON WITH ERNEST TORRENCE TO · · · · · · · · · · · · · ·

Third United Artists Picture of Frozen-Faced Comedian Is River Tale of Old Boats

"Steamboat Bill Jr.," called by many who have seen it, Buster Beaton's funniest comedy, will head the bill at the · Theatre next ·

The frozen-faced funny man who gave us such farces as "College," "The General" and "Go West," now becomes the well-bred son of a burly Mi   sippi River boat captain. When things start going from bad to worse for the father, his "softy" son arrives on the scene. Bill Jr. doesn't exactly give dad any helping hand when he falls in love with the daughter of the rival captain, nor does he help to regain the business which the other has stolen from his father. However, a cyclone comes along and then Buster— but it doesn't require such imagination to think of the antics he indulges in!

Ernest Torrence, featured player in many films since "The Covered Wagon," won a juicy role when he was cast as Buster's he-man parent. It marks his first comedy characterization in many a day. Heading Keaton's supporting cast are Marion Byron, a pretty little newcomer; Tom Lewis, and Tom McGuire.

If you saw "Charley's Aunt" or "The Better 'Ole," you don't need to be told that Charles "Chuck" Reisner is a good comedy director. Why shouldnt he be? His early training was secured at the elbow of Charlie Chaplin!

"Steamboat Bill Jr.," Buster's third comedy for United Artists release, was filmed by Devereaux Jennings and Bert Haines. Carl Harbaugh prepared it as an original screen story. Harry Brand acted in a supervisory capacity.

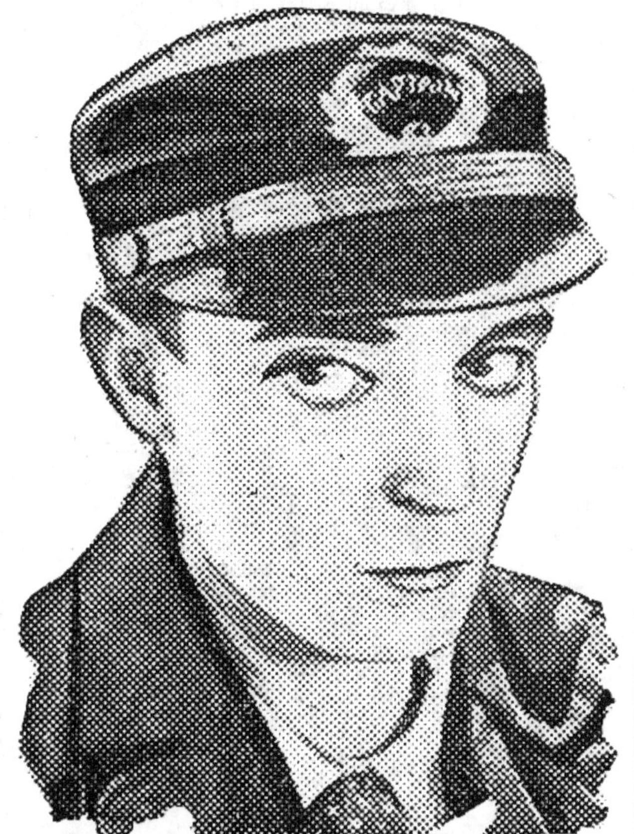

BL-2—One Col. Scene
(Mat 5c; Cut 30c.)

Editors Like Biographies

FILM DIRECTOR WAS
A PRIZE FIGHTER

If life is the greatest teacher, Charles 'Chuck" Reisner, famous director of motion picture comedies, can lay claim to being the world's best educated man.

For the two-fisted, keen-witted builder of screen laughs who was behind the megaphone during the making of the Buster Keaton-Ernest Torrence comedy, "Steamboat Bill, Jr.," which arrives at the ....**next** ...., has crammed into his adventurous career to date experience and success enough for ten men.

Although the amusement world has known Reisner chiefly as a film director during the past few years, a glimpse at his earlier career reveals episodes more exciting than some of the ones he directs for the screen.

Reisner has been a stage hand, stage manager, vaudeville star, professional boxer, successful song writer, motion picture actor, "gag" man, assistant director and director.

Handy with his fists and still handier with his brain, Reisner as a boy became a leader and the one depended upon to take the initiative in any youthful adventure. Growing to manhood, he had a difficult time deciding whether to follow the career of a pugilist or an actor. He rose to stellar heights in both lines, defeating some of the best men of his weight in the ring and winning recognition as a box office bet in vaudeville.

It was while he was following a stage career that he wrote one of the most successful war-time songs, "Good-bye Broadway, Hello France," a popular hit which earned him thousands of dollars for a few hours' work.

Sensing the possibilities of his comedy mind in motion pictures, "Chuck" came, saw and conquered in Hollywood. He was an actor, "gag" man and assistant with Charles Chaplin for several years, and functioned as the great comedian's right hand man during the filming of "The Gold Rush."

Going "on his own" as a full-fledged director, Reisner quickly developed into one of the most popular megaphone wielders. Among his outstanding features before he signed with Keaton were the Syd Chaplin starring vehicles, "The Better 'Ole," "Charley's Aunt" and "The Missing Link."

Buster Keaton who comes to the .... in his latest picture, "Steamboat Bill, Jr.," does not, like the usual comedian, care for so-called funny stories. However, Norman Hapgood confided the following one to him and the frozen-faced comedian broke into one of his rare smiles:

When Hapgood was in Russia, a porter took him to a hotel where he engaged a room. When he returned that evening, he found all his luggage missing. He sent for the porter who said he would go right down and tell Comrade Clerk about this. He did so and Comrade Clerk said, "Comrade Porter, did you take the luggage?" "No," replied Comrade Porter, "Comrade Thief must have taken it."

ERNEST TORRENCE IS
AGAIN A COMEDIAN

Ernest Torrence has gone back to his first love—comedy.

The famous screen villain and character actor has temporarily forsaken the serious roles for a co-starring **part** with Buster Keaton in the United Artists laugh feature, "Steamboat Bill, Jr.," which reaches the.............................. ....Theatre next...........

Born in Edinburgh, Scotland, Torrence was one of a family of fourteen. After attending Edinburgh University, he went to Stuttgart to study piano and vocal music. Returning to Scotland, he became a piano teacher and an amateur singer of note, receiving a medal for his vocal accomplishments.

Deciding to cast his fortunes with the professional stage, he secured an engagement and leaped to fame in Great Britain, where he played in musical shows for fifteen years before coming to America. His first appearance in New York was in "Modest Suzenne." Then followed several musical successes, and it was while he was singing and dancing in "The Night Boat" about eight years ago that Henry King, the director, saw Torrence as a screen possibility.

King was searching for a particularly villainous character for "Tol'able David," the first starring vehicle of Richard Barthelmess. Torrence laughed at first when King approached him with an offer to play a ruffian on the screen, but the director persuaded the comedian that after all, drama and humor are sisters under the skin.

So Torrence played the never-to-be-forgotten role of "Luke" in "Tol'able David" and immediately found several motion picture producers bidding for his services. Particularly will be remembered his roles in "The Covered Wagon," "Ruggles of Red Gap," "The King of Kings," "Twelve Miles Out" and "Captain Salvation."

Several companies were bidding for Torrence's services when he selected the part in "Steamboat Bill Jr." as more to his liking than any role for some time.

"It was a great experience to get back to comedy," said Torrence. "I never had so much fun in my life as when working with Buster and his director, Charles 'Chuck' Reisner."

Torrence is one of the film capital's finest pianists and vocalists, and guests at Hollywood gatherings are always assured of a treat when the noted actor consents to play and sing.

Whether comedian or villain in reel life, he is known as a cultured, home-loving gentleman and a devoted husband and father in real life.

His wife invariably accompanies him on location trips, as she did when the Keaton company spent two months along the Sacramento River filming scenes in the spectacular comedy of river life.

Editors Like Biographies

MARION BYRON IS KEATON LEADING LADY

Unknown a few months ago, without a single day's motion picture experience; now leading lady for one of the most prominent stars and with a five-year contract which should carry her to the heights of fame.

That, in a nutshell, is what the modern Aladdin's lamp—Hollywood—has done for Marion Byron, pint-size comedienne, who plays in Buster Keaton's latest United Artists feature, "Steamboat Bill, Jr.," which is being shown at the.........................Theatre.

Marion, who answers to the unclassical nickname of "Peanuts," is one of the few girls who went to Hollywood and had no idea of breaking into motion pictures. She takes oath that this is the truth.

She was born in Dayton, Ohio, 17 years ago, went to school there, and arrived in Hollywood with her family in 1921. Here she continued her studies. All the films meant to her was an occasional visit to a neighborhood theatre with her playmates. A leader of activities at school, she was always ready for any kind of a lark. One day when the boys invited her to play baseball, she surprised them by batting and running bases as well as any member of the team. When the "gang" gave a "show," Marion ran away with it. But when her friends said: "You should be in the movies," she replied, "Aw, there are too many girls trying to get in them now. I'd rather go on the stage."

About a year ago her family consented, and she won a small bit in a Hollywood musical show. Theatregoers started to talk about her scintillating personality and her rare mimicry. A manager of a number of picture stars persuaded her to have a private screen test "just for a joke." Then, unbeknown to her, he showed the test to Keaton, who was searching high and low for a leading lady.

The next day she visited a studio for the first time and was signed to a five-year contract, appearing with Buster for the first time in "Steamboat Bill, Jr.," under the direction of Charles "Chuck" Reisner.

Buster Keaton, who comes to................ in "Steamboat Bill, Jr.," his latest and third comedy for United Artists, has his own views on what a wife should be. In a recent article, Keaton wrote:

"She must have a lovely smile. She must be able to sing and to cook, and she must never tell funny stories. Under no circumstances must she greet me, when I come home from the studio, with this—'Oh, I saw the funniest thing today, something you can use in your next picture!' The Sullivan Law was put through for people who say that.

"She must love her home and she must be able to put things in it and about it that don't look as though they were put there by an interior decorator. She must be sympathetic, generous and have a decided personality of her own. Also, decided views of her own. She must vote. She must wear soft clothes, with lots of lace and small hats. And she must love children and animals, and a man who never smiles and who sometimes walks downstairs on his head."

FROZEN-FACE MYSTERY EXPLAINED AT LAST

Filmdom's solemnest individual—on the screen—owes his ability to keep a frozen face to his early training on the stage.

Referring, of course, to Buster Keaton, whose immobile visage in "Steamboat Bill Jr.," his latest United Artists comedy, is convulsing audiences at the ....Theatre as never before.

"Be different," they advised, "and you may get some place some day. Anybody can laugh at his own jokes; it's whether audiences laugh that counts in the amusement world."

Keaton's life has been as exciting as his comedies. Although still in his thirties, he has been before the public almost constantly during the past quarter century.

Born on November 4, 1895, during a cyclone, he has enjoyed a cyclonic life ever since. Buster's mother and father, Myra and Joe Keaton, were traveling the country with a tent show, in which the late Harry Houdini, the magician and handcuff king, was a partner.

On the night the stork arrived, a tornado swept that part of Kansas, and away went the show, tent and all. The only building left standing was a church, and there Mrs. Keaton was taken. Buster was born in the sacristy.

When the Keaton offspring was six months old he fell downstairs—and seemed to enjoy the experience.

"What a buster!" exclaimed Houdini.

"That's a good name for the kid," opined Joe Keaton, and Buster it has been to this day.

After Houdini and the elder Keaton dissolved partnership, "Dad" Keaton and his wife organized a vaudeville set. Buster joined them at the age of three and during the next sixteen years he visited every city in the United States and the British colonies.

Buster turned down a $750 a week at Shubert's Winter Garden in New York to enter motion pictures at $40 a week in 1916. Early in 1917 the comedian—

He was then given his own company by Mr. Schenck. His first picture, "One Week," proved a big success Overnight he became a box office attraction and his "frozen face" brought him world-wide fame.

Some of the most successful feature length comedies made by Buster Keaton during the past few years are "Three Ages," "Hospitality," Sherlock, Junior," "The Navigator," "Seven Chances," "Go West," "Battling Butler," "The General" and "College." "Steamboat Bill Jr." is his latest.

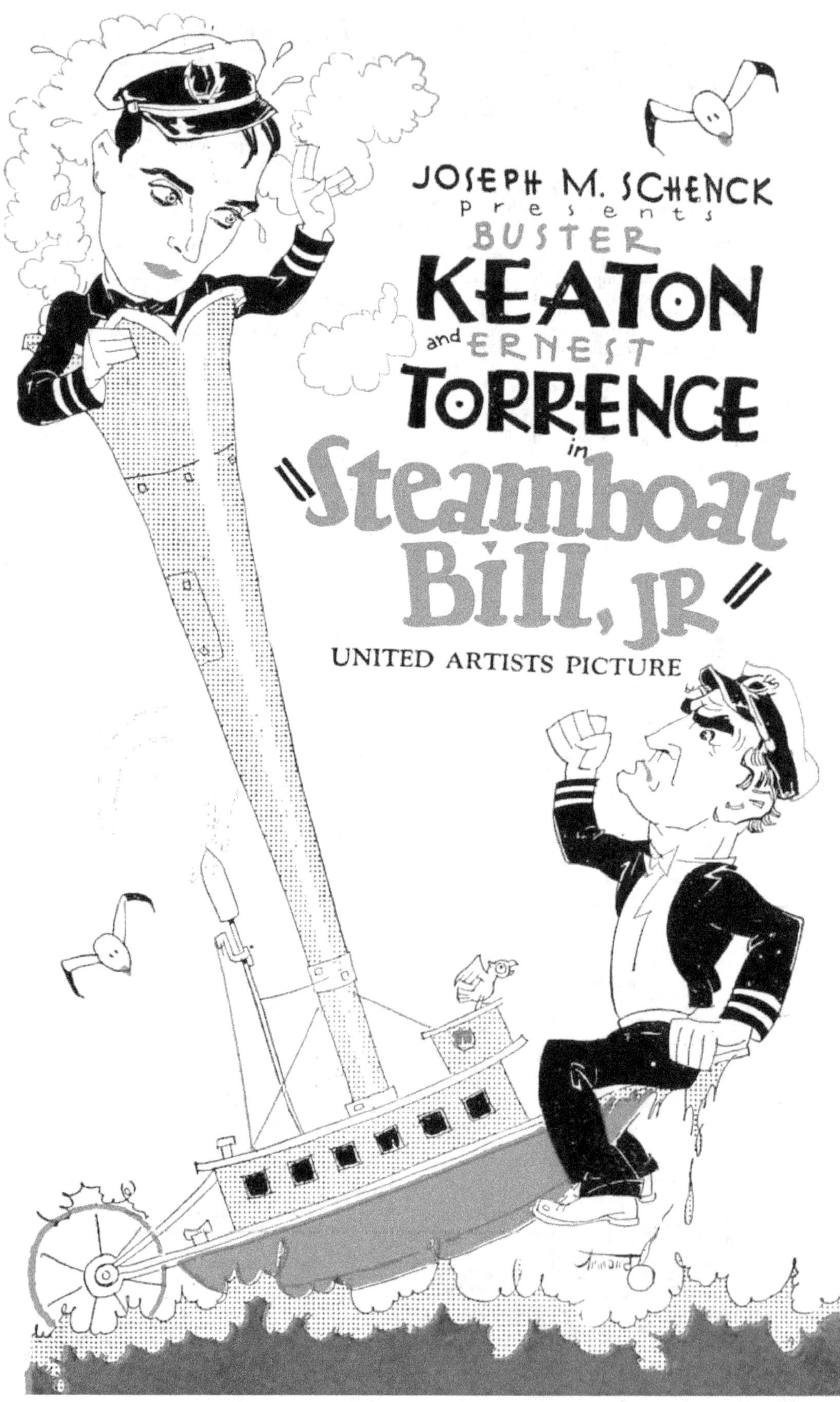
JOSEPH M. SCHENCK
presents
BUSTER
KEATON
and ERNEST
TORRENCE
in
"Steamboat Bill, Jr"
UNITED ARTISTS PICTURE

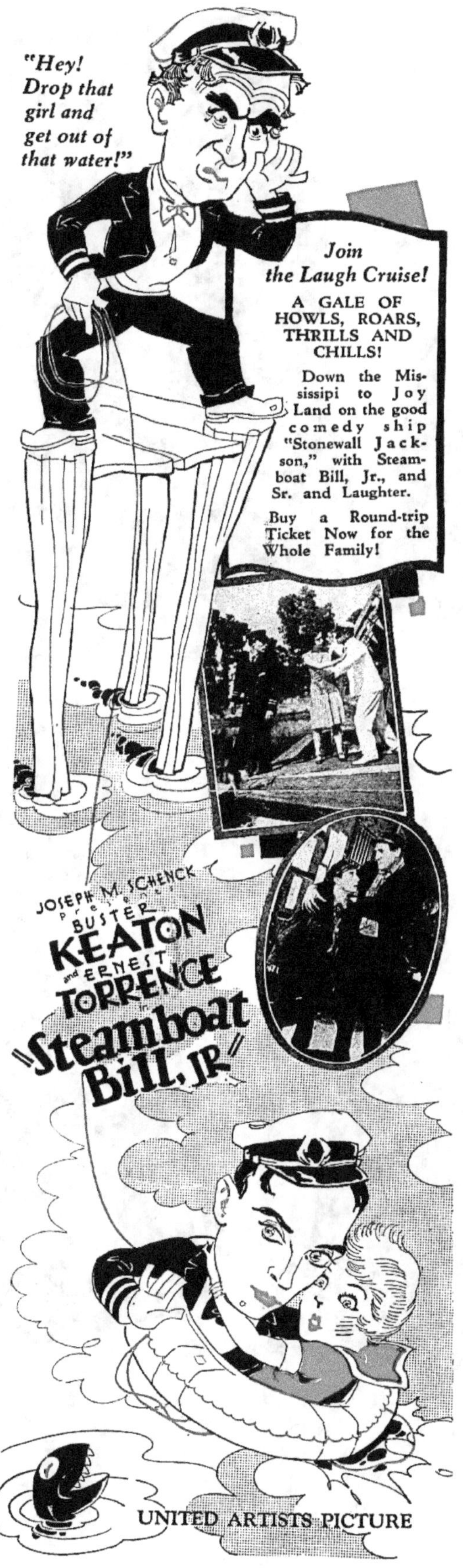
"Hey! Drop that girl and get out of that water!"
Join the Laugh Cruise!
A GALE OF HOWLS, ROARS, THRILLS AND CHILLS!
Down the Mississipi to Joy Land on the good comedy ship "Stonewall Jackson," with Steamboat Bill, Jr., and Sr. and Laughter.
Buy a Round-trip Ticket Now for the Whole Family!
JOSEPH M. SCHENCK presents
BUSTER KEATON and ERNEST TORRENCE in
"Steamboat Bill, Jr."
UNITED ARTISTS PICTURE

POSTERS

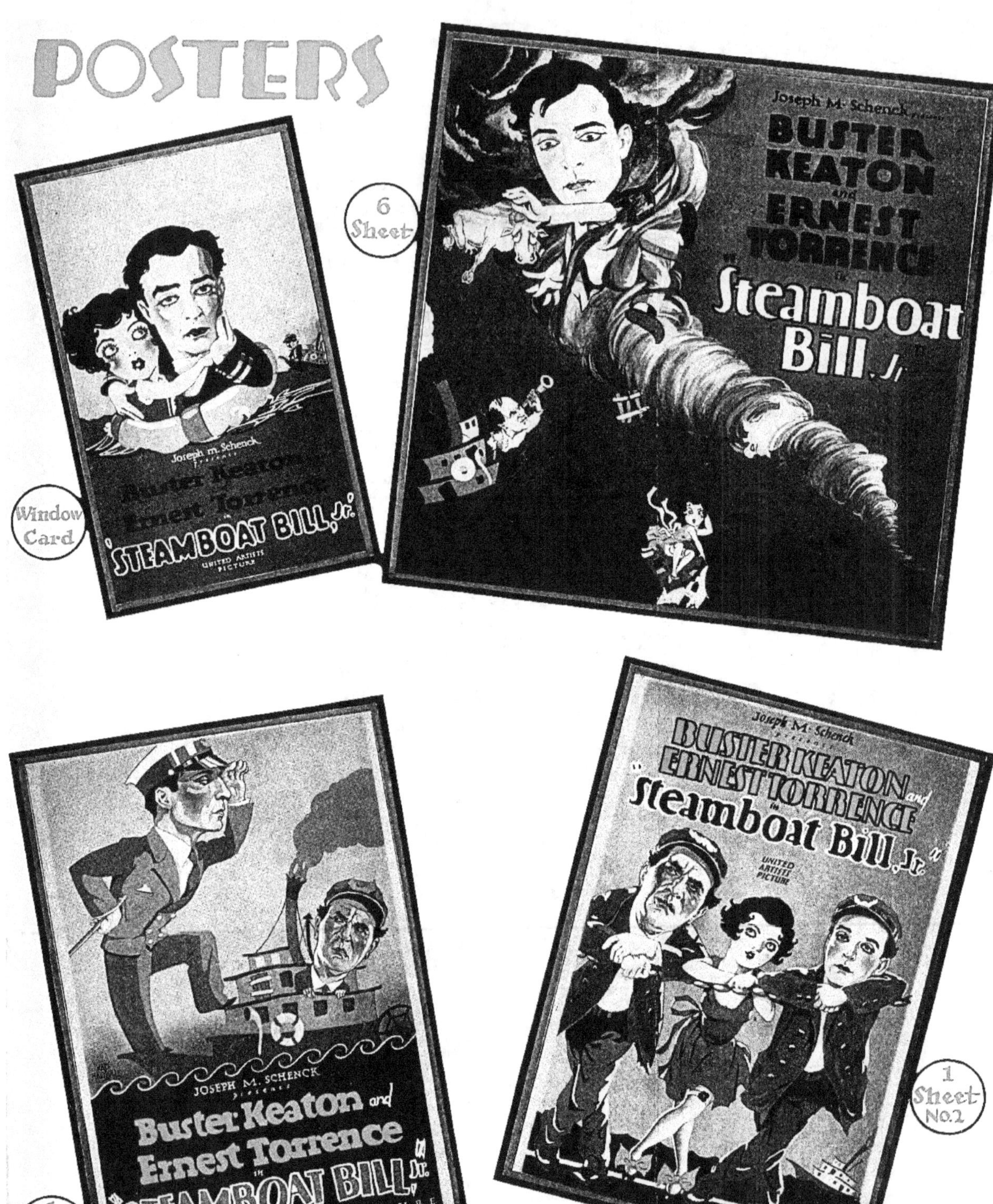

ABOUT THE COLLECTIONS

Movie Publicity Showcase is made up of poster and press materials from many collections, including the author's. Sadly, most of this material is in private hands and is generally not available to the fan, researcher, or collector, except at exuberant prices if and when these items can be found.

Ironically the material was intended for public consumption. Theaters could use the stories and images to drive interest in the films and increase attendance at showings.

Movie Publicity Showcase makes this material available once again for the first time in decades from original sources. It is hoped that these ads and publicity stories will lead to the further desire to watch and collect the movies, many available today on DVD.

Classic Hollywood deserves to live on!

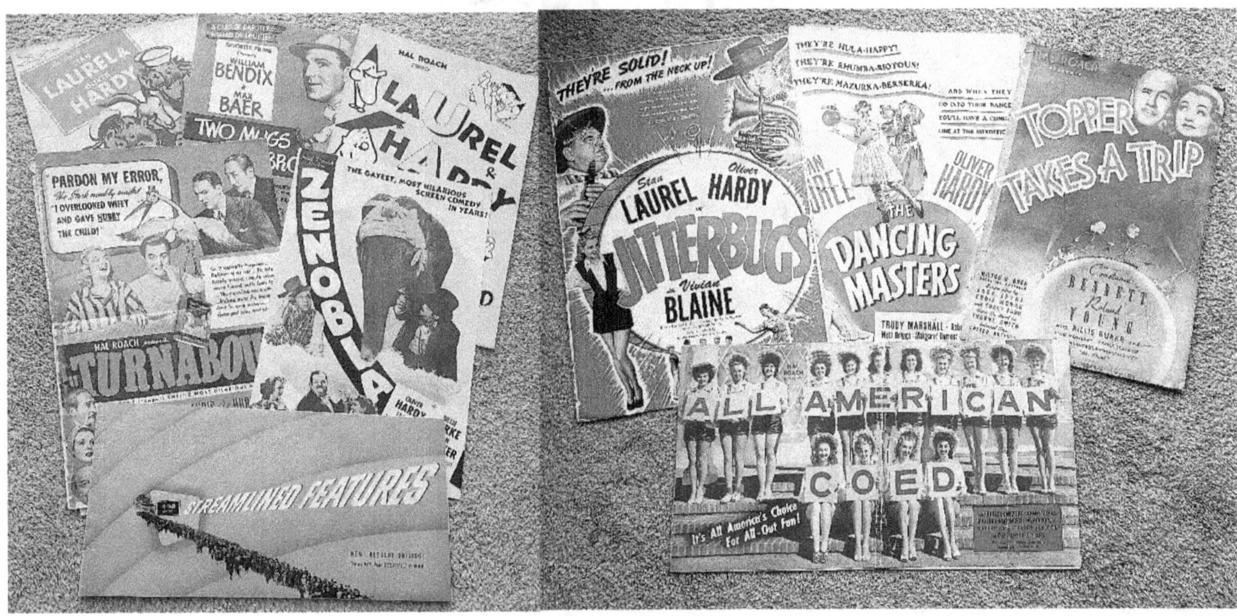

ABOUT THE AUTHOR

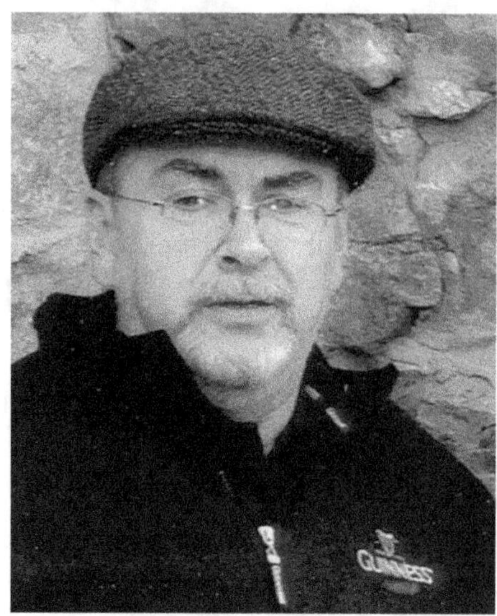

I. Joseph Hyatt is an entertainment archeologist/author. A member of the Sons of the Desert, the Laurel and Hardy Appreciation Society, Hyatt's articles and books have been printed internationally. Traveling across the US, and drawing on many collections, including his own, his books bring back past eras with words and photographs.

I. Joseph Hyatt currently serves as the Vice-President of the Board of Trustees for the Union County Performing Arts Center of New Jersey, a fully restored 1928 movie/vaudeville palace.